HANK THE YANK
DOWN UNDER

Adventures in Oz

Chris Wallace

In the spirit of reconciliation, Round Lake Publishing acknowledges the Traditional Custodians of country throughout Australia and their connections to land, sea and community. We pay our respect to their Elders past and present and extend that respect to all Aboriginal and Torres Strait Islander peoples today.

ISBN: 978-0-6459687-5-0

Published by Round Lake Publishing
Book cover design by Rainsford
Book design by Jana Lulovska
Back cover photo by Brett Tucker

This book is dedicated with love beyond words to my one and only **A.**

CONTENTS

FORWARD

Nora Ephron's mother famously told her daughter, "Everything is copy." I agree 100% and live by that credo. Anyone who knows me knows I love to tell stories. That's what this book is: stories. The first story in this book is about a visit to Australia in the 1960s, long before I ever dreamed I'd come here to live. The last story in this book <u>began</u> in the 1960s, but ends in 2025. That was quite accidental, but I like the synchronicity of it. It makes it appear as if I meant to. I didn't. It just turned out that way.

I came here to live in 1994. I had my sixtieth birthday two months after I arrived. You do the math. That's not usually when a person starts a new life in a new country. Hell, that's not even when a person does much of anything if they're in their right mind. You can draw your own conclusions on that one too.

It wasn't long before serendipity and the unexpected found me here, just as it has all my life. Things just tended to happen and the next thing you know I was living a life here that was as full of surprises as my previous lives in St. Louis and Ohio and New York and the Army and Hollywood and every other place I've ever been. So let's begin, with the understanding that I'm not nearly clever enough to make this stuff up.

*But first, I'll explain the name Hank the Yank. I never expected to have an acting career here, but early in the piece, I was asked to be in a play at LaMama, then I was cast in an outdoor production of **The Great Gatsby** and in a television show called **The Genie from Down Under** on the ABC. On that show, you heard me before you saw me. Off camera you heard, "Eeeeeeeeee-haw!!!" Then the camera found me and I said, "How y'all doin'? I'm Hank the Yank!"*

FIRST TIME OVER THE RAINBOW

I found myself with a unique opportunity. I was separated but not yet divorced from a woman who worked for a major American airline. We were on excellent terms. My wanderlust had already taken me to Africa and the Middle East, the latter trip we had taken together. Now, we were no longer living as husband and wife but stayed in touch and remained friendly.

During one of our regular phone conversations, we talked about my taking a trip.

"Where would you go if you could get away for a few weeks?" she asked.

"I don't know. I haven't thought about it," I answered.

"Well, why don't you think about it? We're still married and you're entitled to a discount on other airlines as my husband. You won't have many opportunities like this."

"True," I said. "And I probably won't have too many wives who would be that generous."

"I'm not being generous," she laughed. "It's my employer who has the connections. Why not use them?"

"Where could I go that would be interesting?" I wondered aloud.

"Well, we've seen the Middle East and Greece. You've been to Africa. You saw Europe when you were in the army. What's left?" she asked.

I thought for a moment. "Australia, I guess. That might be interesting."

That's how simply the wheels were set in motion for my first visit to what was a number of years later to become my home.

I was living in New York at the time and working at the local NBC station, WNBC-TV producing on-air promotion. Airline employees and their immediate family were shown enormous courtesies between carriers. As a result, it would not have been unusual to get an upgrade to first class on a ticket which was issued at a 90% discount. It was also unnecessary to book each step of one's journey. If your flight was booked, let's say, from New York to Los Angeles, you could schedule stops in Chicago, Denver or wherever you wanted along the way at no additional cost and pretty much deplane and reboard at will, subject only to availability which was usually no problem.

The flight that I booked had stops in Los Angeles and Honolulu. I flew the first leg with no discomfort. By the time I reached Honolulu, however, I felt as though I'd been sitting for days. The flight to Sydney was going to be enough additional hours that I opted to spend the night in Honolulu and continue on the next day. I knew that the flight would not be booked out because none ever was, making stand-by flying a cinch.

The weather in Hawaii was as it always is: perfect. I hadn't had much sleep the night before departing and was too groggy to really enjoy myself. But I found a hotel room with a bar nearby. After a couple of beers, I took a walk along the beach in a half-daze. Finally, at around 8 a.m. New York time, I forced myself to go to bed. I had reached that point when you're so tired you can hardly stand up but too tired to sleep when you lie down. It seemed as though too much was taking place too quickly for me to assimilate it all and my brain was lagging behind, trying twice as hard to catch up. My exhaustion eventually won out and I slept like a rock.

Later that day, Wednesday, after a leisurely breakfast I went for another walk along Waikiki beach. This falls into the "some things never change" category, but on this my first visit, I had heard so much about how Waikiki had lost all its charm and resembled Miami Beach more and more. Miami Beach, at that time, was thought of as so crassly commercial that no one could like it except retired New Yorkers. I found Waikiki to be so naturally beautiful that it didn't matter that there may have been hotels there too. People who go there today long for the good old days when I was first there, when it wasn't so crassly commercial as it is now. Some folks just don't like to see anything change. I took in all this tropical beauty without prejudice, then moseyed to the airport. Predictably, there was no problem and the airline personnel took very good care of me.

As I boarded the plane and made the way to my assigned seat, I noticed a rather large man sprawled across two seats, virtually occupying them both without effort. He looked like the kind of guy who not only enjoys but also expects his creature comforts. The plane wasn't full so he had no reluctance about taking up all the space he needed. He hadn't yet taken off his gray Stetson hat which was perched down near the top of his huge glasses, making his eyes look as big as an owl's. His manner was easy and he gave me a smile as I passed. I nodded back.

Later, after we'd had a meal and still had a matter of hours to fly, I was stretching my legs near the galley. Doug lumbered up.

"On your way to Sydney?" he asked.

"Yes I am," I answered.

"Give me a coke, would you, honey," he said to the flight attendant, then turned to me. "You been in Australia before?"

"No, this is my first time," I replied.

"Here on business?" he asked.

"No. Just for a look around,"

That could have ended the conversation. As I considered this option, I also realized that there was a lot of time to kill. "Where are you from in the states?" I asked.

"A little town in Indiana," he answered.

"Where abouts? I have an uncle who lives in Indiana."

It turned out that he lived in a tiny town just nine miles from the lake where my uncle lived and where I'd spent countless summers. His town was where we went shopping for groceries.

"Come on. Let's sit down and talk," he suggested. I followed him back to his seat and after he spread himself out, I wedged into the remaining space.

He was on his way to his cattle station, which I learned was the same as a cattle ranch except the noun and location were different. His was located in the Northern Territory, the real Outback, the Bush.

"I'm going to be in Brisbane until Thursday," he told me. "If you don't have anything better to do, give me a call and meet me there and we'll fly to Mt. Isa together. Then we'll get a little puddle jumper for the trip to Borroloola. I'll have my private plane pick us up there. That's the nearest landing strip to where my cattle station is. Come on up. We're having a muster."

"A muster?" I asked.

"Yeah, a round-up is called a muster in Australia. And mustangs are called brumbys. But we'll be mustering cattle."

"What do they call cattle in Australia?" I asked.

"Cattle," he said, giving me a look that asked, *what else would they call them?*

"I'll think about it and let you know," I said. The idea of getting to that part of Australia was very appealing. Since I lived in New York City, any other city was going to pale by comparison, particularly an Australian city. And I didn't come all this way just to see another city. I wanted to see the country and meet the people. Only a couple of years before I had been in East Africa where I spent my time with people who lived there. It's the only way to really experience another country.

We arrived in Sydney on Friday night, losing a day crossing the International Date Line. I had made no plans or reservations prior to arrival except to allow my adventure to unfold however it would. An airport bus took me into the city.

After asking a couple of people for suggestions as to where I might stay, I was directed to Kings Cross. I had no knowledge of or expectations about this colorful part of Sydney. I knew nothing of its history or sexual orientation. I didn't know anything beyond the fact that, according to my sources, it was a happening spot and I was a single man. The Kings Cross Hotel seemed to be a decent enough place so I took a room and settled in. The Kings Cross that I experienced at that time was a mere suggestion of what one would experience today. It was lively to be sure but didn't have any of the seediness it has now. Or maybe it did and I didn't notice.

As soon as I walked out onto the street for a look around, I was struck by a few things. First of all, there seemed to be a hippie population not essentially different than I'd seen in New York, Mykonos and elsewhere. The uniforms were the same everywhere: beads, sandals, jeans, tie-dyes, tee shirts, mini-skirts, headbands, shoulder bags. Their hair was frizzy, long, straight, in braids or hanging free. Everyone on the planet belonged to what appeared to be one world culture, all dressed by the same designer, Australia being no exception. Before the Internet and all the technology we enjoy today which shortens the distances between people, there was the hippie culture which, in its own unique way, did the same thing, connecting the world without benefit of technology. Peace and love dominated, at least in theory.

Also, having come from New York, I was prepared for most anything on the streets. But I wasn't quite prepared for the openness and campiness of the gay community I encountered at the Cross, both male and female. It took me quite aback. I hadn't had a lot of contact at that time and, therefore, my reference point was narrow. I found it interesting but not in any way threatening. I was amused more than anything else. I saw one guy who made me laugh. He was dressed in women's shorty pajamas, wore silver boots and a large chain around one leg. He minced down the street with purpose, feigning indifference to the impression he was making, but smug with the reality of it, completely in his own world. If the expression had been in my vocabulary at the time, I'd have said, "On ya, mate."

The weather was quite warm on Saturday so I decided to go to the beach. I asked at the front desk where I should go and how to get there.

"Take the bus out front here that says Bondi Beach on it and go to the very last stop," the clerk told me. "That's our most famous beach and I reckon it'd be the one for you."

Even though it was before noon, the beach was already crowded. It reminded me of Jones Beach in the heart of summer in New York except that the atmospheric conditions were unique. I had been told about the way the light created such an unusual sharpness in Sydney. I had observed a similar phenomenon in Athens and San Francisco. But nothing prepared me for the brilliance of that November day at Bondi Beach. It nearly hurt one's eyes it was so clear. The only other time I've experienced anything like it was playing Frisbee one day at Will Rogers homestead in Pacific Palisades; except that time my crystal clear perception was aided by some special mushrooms.

I found a place on the powdery sand, threw down my hotel towel, took off my tee shirt, spread out and opened my book. It was hard to concentrate on literature when there were so many new things to observe. Instead, I spent the time looking around at the people who immediately surrounded me, the surfers who were riding the waves off shore and the small boats with their sails unfurled out on the distant horizon.

In my periphery, a long mane of cascading red hair accompanied by a white bikini demanded my immediate attention. *Holy fucking Toledo*, I said to myself. In most instances, a bikini is in place to hold things up. In this case, the bikini was merely resting comfortably over a beautiful pair of ample, generous breasts. Below were a flat stomach, athletic legs and a nicely shaped butt. This was an authentic Aussie sheila.

Without waiting to consider an alternative, I gathered up my stuff and wound my way back toward the street; then walked toward her and her friend as if I'd just arrived at the beach. I located myself in a space close enough that a conversation could easily develop. I couldn't help paying a lot of attention to them – well, to her anyway.

As discreetly as possible I looked in her direction, hoping to make some kind of eye contact. It would have been rude to stare even though it's all I wanted to do.

I found, however, that my glances were being returned by her far less interesting girlfriend. Each time I would look in her direction, my eyes would be met by the girlfriend's. I pretended to read my book, waiting for an opportunity to say something.

Finally the girlfriend announced loud enough for me to hear, "I think I'll go in the water and cool off a bit" and shot a not very subtle glance my way. I half-smiled in return, hoping that she would take it as a clue that I'd be right behind her.

As soon as she'd cleared the area, I made my lame move.

"Would you mind looking up and smiling and saying hello?"

The look on her face told me how pathetic my attempt had been. She spoke no words and barely directed her disinterest at me, as if she couldn't even be bothered doing that.

I was committed by now and tried again. "I was told that Australians are very friendly people and welcome Americans with open arms."

She looked up from her newspaper and into my eyes. "I'm sorry," she said with a slightly pained look on her face, then returned to her paper.

"You mean I've come all this way for nothing, that it's all a lie?"

This time when she looked up her expression was not quite so severe. She seemed to examine me for a long moment before indicating anything. Her better nature – from my standpoint – took over. With a kind of resignation which might have discouraged anyone else, she sighed and asked, "Where do you come from?"

"New York. I just got in last night."

The ice was broken and by the time the girlfriend returned, soaking wet, it was clear where my real intentions lay, in a manner of speaking.

We all three chatted away. I wasn't sure if I was being treated courteously or if something was actually happening between Rose and me. As we discussed nothing in particular, and as a kind of distraction, Rose began drawing the outline of a house in the sand. Together we created a fantasy couple who lived there. I made jokes about what he did for a living and tried my best to be ever so amusing and clever until Rose began describing the layout of the house.

"This is the kitchen," she said in her beautifully modulated and well-educated voice. "She always has some homemade bikkies for her man."

"Bikkies?"

"Biscuits."

"Biscuits?" I knew biscuits as something you eat with gravy or butter and jam.

"Yes. I think you call them cookies," she replied. She continued her tour of the house. "This is the lounge room where they watch the telly. And this is their bedroom where they make love." She looked up into my eyes at that moment.

Another *Holy fucking Toledo* came to mind. But while I was holy Toledo-ing, I still didn't know how to proceed. There was the girlfriend and I couldn't ask them to come back to my hotel. So I did what every idiot does in that kind of situation: nothing.

By now the sun had lost most of its power and it was late afternoon. We had continued talking and laughing and having a lovely time with no promise of anything more. All I knew were their names.

"I've had enough sun for today," Rose said to her friend.

"Me too. Shall we go?" the friend asked.

"I think so," Rose answered and began gathering her things and putting them in a woven straw bag.

I was still tongue-tied and without a clue as to what to do next when Rose looked up at me. "Would you like to come with us and have a chop?"

"A chop?" I asked.

"Yes, a bite to eat," she explained.

"Oh, yeah, that'd would be great," I answered with enormous relief.

They gave me a lift back to the hotel and waited while I had a quick shower. This was another thing which endeared me to Australia from the very beginning. In Europe you'd have been lucky to find one of those hand shower gadgets in the bathroom of any place I could afford. Other places where I'd been would not even have that distant relative to our American necessity. Usually it was a tub and that's all. The British in particular seemed to find a tub more than adequate. But here there were proper showers that you could stand under with hands free to do their work.

We arrived at Rose's home in the late afternoon, bordering on early evening. Light was leaving the sky and a cool darkness was descending. Rose lit several candles and placed them around the lounge room. Next, some mellow jazz added to the atmosphere. Her friend was very much at home in this house and went about preparing some dinner, while Rose handed me a bottle of red wine and a corkscrew.

Sitting around the table was more of the same kind of flirtation and innuendo that we'd engaged in at Bondi. With the friend there, it had to be limited to talk and anything further had to remain hypothetical. Like many members of the male sex, I had no real idea whether or not I was making any headway. I needed very positive, unmistakable signs. None was forthcoming. At least none that I detected. It may have seemed like I was playing it cool but the truth was I didn't know whether to shit or wind my watch, as the saying goes.

After we'd had some ice cream and coffee and too much wine, the friend decided that it was time to go. She asked me if I needed a lift back to the hotel.

"Oh, I'll give him a ride later," Rose said. "You're in no hurry, are you?"

"No," I answered. 'I'm on holiday and there's nothing on my dance card until next Thursday at the earliest."

The friend left. Rose and I picked up our wine glasses and she led me into a smaller lounge room, the most prominent feature of which was a kind of day bed. We talked about nothing and then talked about nothing a little more. It was one vamp after another. I had been out of circulation for all practical purposes since separating from my airline wife and wasn't sure exactly how to approach a woman I found as attractive as I found Rose.

Whether what happened next was an indication of my pathetic behavior or whether it was an indication of what Aussie women were like, Rose took charge. She got a devilish smile on her face.

"Are you really as good as you think you are?"

The question stunned me. I wasn't feeling particularly good at anything at that moment. "What do you mean?"

"You know what I mean. Are you the lover you appear to be?"

Aha! That was a sign! Even I could figure that one out. The synapses were firing. "I guess we'll just have to find out, won't we?" I said. It felt like a line from a movie but it was the best I could come up with.

That began a sexual encounter which lasted throughout my time in Australia. At every available moment we were naked somewhere, either at her place or at my hotel. We spent every night together even though she was working during the day. I spent my time away from Rose doing something I'm sure, but what it may have been is a dark mystery. I basically existed from one sexual moment to the next.

Whatever insecurities I may have had about women after the breakup of my marriage were dispelled for the duration of my time in Oz. Rose could no more get enough of me than I could of her. We were both absolutely voracious.

In addition to all the personal pleasure she provided, Rose became my tour guide. We went to dinner at one quaint little restaurant after another. The variety in the cuisine wasn't nearly what it is now. But there were places that were still quite charming.

At this one little bistro, we were there at its most popular time. One table of about eight had a woman who was absolutely stunning. She was wearing a long, black, spaghetti strapped dress, had short cropped dark hair and the face of a movie star. She was so elegant and poised and fun-loving and charming and feminine that she totally dominated her little group. When she went onto the little dance floor with a partner, she glided like silk and at intervals confidently gave her partner a flirtatious peck on the cheek. I was mesmerized.

Rose saw how taken I was with this woman and smiled. When my eyes re-focused on her I asked, "What are you smiling at? You're not jealous, are you?"

Her face lit up as she laughed and stared at me.

"What?" I asked.

"That's a bloke," she said.

"A what?"

"A bloke," she repeated.

"A bloke?"

"Yes, a guy, a man," she smiled.

"You're kidding me," I protested.

"No, love, it's a bloke. Fair dinkum."

I looked again and was no better able to verify or argue than I had been before. Even then Australia was not at all self-conscious about homosexuality or other sexual differences. Tolerance is part of the Australian character, as natural as a kangaroo is to the Bush. The openness of it, the lack of comment about it all was both wonderfully foreign and at the same time beautifully refreshing to me. I could only think that it wouldn't have been the case if we were in Des Moines.

My time with Rose was bliss but I didn't want to miss the opportunity that Doug had provided me. Once I was assured that Rose would be there when I returned, I left Sydney.

I arrived in Brisbane on Thursday afternoon. In my own excitement about arriving in Australia the previous Friday, I hadn't noticed a phenomenon that should have been obvious. At the airport in Brisbane I was aware of the festive atmosphere and gaiety that surrounded me. Until you've made the trip, you don't realize how isolated Australia is from the world most of its immigrants once knew. Even today you can feel as though you have little direct connection to the rest of the planet. At that time, it was even more so. People were arriving from all over the globe, greeted by relatives and loved ones who may not have seen them in years. Or they may have been family members returning from the mandatory overseas trip. All non-indigenous Australians think about going overseas because that's where all their roots are. Laughter and screams of joy filled the terminal. Then a look in another direction would reveal such a profound sadness that it was palpable. Someone was leaving. Those left behind wore heartbreaking expressions and tear-stained faces. These great distances create strong emotions. In other parts of the world, parents rue the day when their children go twenty-five miles away to college. Imagine what it must have been like for Australian parents to see their children off to places oceans away.

Doug had made a reservation for me at the hotel where he was staying, a comfortable, unpretentious and well used facility. The plan was to leave the next day.

After a certain amount of errand running, we boarded the plane for Mt. Isa, a community of about 15,000 people whose principal industry was copper mining. The flight was uncomplicated and before long we were descending. As we approached the landing field, it was obvious that this scrub country was spare indeed, red and burnt out. Then my eyes were attracted to a patch of bright green. It defied logic to look down on this isolated country and see this aberration. It was like a huge emerald resting in a sea of ground cinnamon.

"What's that?" I asked.

Without seeming to take any notice, Doug said, "Looks like a cricket pitch."

It brings to mind another similar experience a friend told me about a few years later. He had been assigned to the Saigon bureau of NBC News as assistant bureau chief. The war had been waging for some time by then. As his plane was approaching Saigon, he could clearly see the devastation of the entire countryside, burnt beyond recognition by napalm. Suddenly a sea of lush, green vegetation came into view. It didn't belong with the rest of the landscape. When he asked what it could possibly be, he was told that it was the Michelin rubber plantation. Both sides in the conflict were sufficiently paid off to keep them from destroying business. Three cheers for capitalism.

We stretched our legs for a minute before boarding another plane, this one much smaller with four reciprocating engines. Doug and I climbed aboard along with two very smartly dressed young women and a box of baby chicks. After listening to the drone of jet engines on my previous flights, propellers and cheeping chicks created an interesting cacophony all the way to Borroloola in the Northern Territory.

Doug's pilot was there when we arrived, his Cessna 180 all fueled and ready to go. Borroloola was a dusty little crossroads made up of a police station, a general store, a school for Aboriginal children and a couple of other buildings. These modest structures and its negligible population, nevertheless, were entitled to identification on the maps of Australia.

A note on the little pad that I carried with me said it all: Now the adventure really begins. We arrived at the old homestead, a rustic area that housed Colin, the head stockman, his wife and a couple of small children; Old Col, an ancient of undetermined age whose principal function seemed to be to watch things (what he watched was never disclosed); Holly, a very attractive 20-something-year-old woman originally from California whose husband, Jock, was a crop-duster with all the swagger and devil-may-care attitude of a top gun, crooked smile, the whole package. There was also an Aboriginal family living at the old homestead that appeared to be completely integrated into that tight little society. The cattle operation was run from here.

Doug had told them in advance that he was bringing a guest for a visit. I don't know how he may have described me but whatever he said certainly resulted in general curiosity. They all wanted to have a look at this greenhorn from New York City.

Holly baked a lemon pie that she'd been saving up for and preparing for three weeks. We had it with our tea. She seemed especially glad to have another Yank to talk to. I either got the impression or created it in my mind, that Jock was less accessible than she would have liked. I knew I was treading on frontier land that had its own morals and ethics so I didn't pursue anything more than the most superficial conversation.

After tea we hopped back into the Cessna 180 and flew to the Bessie, as the new homestead was called. It consisted of a series of unfinished buildings and several house trailers, or caravans, for family men. Piles of lumber and miles of tubing and wiring were scattered about the area indicating that construction was well underway and ongoing. There were a number of wooden frames with corrugated metal around the sides and burlap stretched overhead to keep the direct sunlight away. The kitchen facility was the principal one of these. The red dust was ankle deep and puffed around your boots as you walked from one site to another. The most colorful character of this construction mob was Tom the Cook. He was too old to labor along with the others and had no doubt inherited the cooking chores by default. Like Old Col back at the old homestead, Tom the Cook was toothless except for a canine tooth on the upper right side of his mouth and another tooth on the left lower. It gave his smile a picturesque quality that he happily displayed whenever the occasion arose.

Tom the Cook loved to talk. We had been told at the old homestead that the temperature had reached 109 that afternoon (Australia hadn't converted to Celsius yet). Someone brought that fact to Tom the Cook's attention.

"Hundred and bloody nine? Hundred and bloody nine my auntie's bloody britches. It was a hundred and bloody fifteen at the crack o' dawn and got up to a hundred and bloody forty by midday. Didn't even have to fire up the bloody stove to cook bloody eggs it was so bloody hot. Y'ever seen it so hot, Yank?"

"Can't say that I have," I answered.

Doug pointed out the shower to me. It was fifty feet away from the cooking area and consisted of what looked like part of an old curved piece of metal that water flowed into from a water tower above it. That, in turn, fed into a can that had holes punched in the bottom. A small metal chain was pulled to get the water to flow onto the showier. It was entirely an open-air affair. No room for modesty amongst these blokes.

"We don't have a lot of water here so don't think you're in New York City. Best to get wet, lather up and then rinse it off," Doug said.

"You won't need a bloody towel to dry off. This heat'll dry you off in a bloody minute," Tom the Cook added.

I had stowed my gear under a cot that was set up in an open area. In a few minutes I was under the shower counting the drops of water I used.

"How's the water, mate?" Tom the Cook called out, "Wet?"

I nodded.

"The water's wet, is it? Been so dry up here for so long you can't expect too bloody much. Wet, is it?" He chuckled to himself and started preparing the evening meal.

A full moon was rising as we gathered around the tables. Many of the men working as laborers spoke a limited brand of English. They were mostly Italians who had come to Australia looking for a better life. We sat down to a plate of top roast beef, tomatoes, onions, beets and freshly made bread, a feast in any man's language.

"Ever eat Gallah?" Tom the Cook asked.

"What's that?" I asked.

"You've seen these bloody pink birds flyin' around here, haven't ya?"

"Are they like parrots?" I asked.

"That's them," he answered. "Ever eat one?" I shook my head. "Them bloody birds is a delicacy up here in the Northern Territory."

"Really?"

"Bloody oath, mate. But you got to know how to cook 'em."

"How do you cook them?" I asked, thinking I was being polite and not knowing that I'd just taken Tom the Cook's bait.

"Well, they's gotta be cooked with minerals. That's the only bloody way to eat them. What you do is put 'em in a big pot with a large stone, bloody rock really. Then you boil them together for as long as it bloody takes. Then when the stone is soft, you eat it and throw the bloody bird away." He could hardly get the story out before he erupted with laughter, displaying his broad, two-toothed smile. "When the stone's soft, you eat it and throw the bloody bird away! That's a good 'un. Eat the bloody stone and throw the bloody bird away!" With each repetition he slapped the table with his palm and flashed both his teeth.

Later, I stretched out on my cot and looked up at the endless sky above me. In some gum trees nearby I heard some cackling and banging going on. I couldn't tell what was making the racket. Doug's cot was near mine.

"What's that noise?" I asked.

"Those are flying foxes," he answered.

"Flying foxes?"

"They're huge bats, could be the biggest in the world."

"What do they feed on?" I asked cautiously.

"Insects, I think. Maybe some fruit," he answered. He looked at me over the top of his glasses. "They're not vampires," he smiled.

The moon was bright enough to read by. Since I wasn't yet sleepy, I took out the book I traveled with and opened it. As I looked at the words, nothing registered. My mind traveled back to an evening in Uganda.

I was spending the night in a modest hotel on the outskirts of Kampala, from which I'd be leaving next morning for a camp at Murchison Falls. As I stood on the balcony, looking out over the little park across the street, I noticed what looked like a black line stringing up from way off in the distance to my left, climbing into the sky and widening as it climbed. The black line became a ribbon and kept widening and widening until it was a great swath streaking across the evening sky. Soon a sound accompanied the ribbon as it made its way through the sky in front of me on its way to an unknown destination to my right. The sky became blackened with this enormous quivering ribbon. It was a massive, incalculable number of bats. There must have been millions of them. Where they came from and where they were headed only they knew. But the impact they made on the tranquility of that night sky was immense. Although much smaller in numbers, these Australian cousins were equally impressive in their own way as they banged around the trees near my bed.

Next morning, just after dawn, the Bessie came alive. Doug had a day planned for me that would begin soon after breakfast. As we approached the tables, Tom the Cook was still amusing himself with the Galah story, hashing it and re-hashing it and then hashing it once more. It's easy to imagine how profound events impact a remote society that is relatively stable and where there's a familiar routine. Anything out of the ordinary becomes amplified as it is repeated and repeated until it passes into legend and takes on mythic importance. Just think of Biblical legends or other oral histories which have moved down from generation to generation over the ages. In my own family, on my mother's side, we are to have descended from Constantine XI, the last emperor of the Byzantine Empire. The legend has passed down through the generations, not written anywhere but no less valid or possible. Somebody must have told somebody back then until here I am writing about it. Tom the Cook's Galah story may not have that long lasting potential, but he was giving it his best shot.

Breakfast was tea, some freshly baked bread and butter and a piece of what was referred to as steak. I chewed it for a while on one side of my mouth, then chewed it some more on the other side, tried the first side again until my jaw got tired and finally opted to swallow it as it was and let my stomach work it out. How Tom the Cook managed that leathery mass with his limited dental capacity, I can't imagine.

We flew up to the old homestead where Doug was going to deplane and Holly was going to join me for a visit to a neighbor. The distances are so vast in the Northern Territory that the only efficient way to go from one cattle station to another is by air. Doug told me when we were approaching the Bessie that his station was thousands and thousands of square miles in area and that he'd never seen all of it, even from the air.

While we were enroute, Holly and I had a chance to talk.

"What's it like for you, stuck up here in the middle of nowhere?" I asked

She thought for a moment. "What I like most is the security," she said simply.

"Security?"

"Yeah," she answered. "You don't have to worry about food. There's shelter. No doctor bills ."

"What do you mean, no doctor bills?" I asked.

"We have the medical service. It comes to us," she said, then added, "No insurance man comes around to collect every week. I don't know. I just love it." She looked down at the desolate country we were floating over. With total serenity on her face she looked at me again. "I keep the books for Doug so I feel like I'm doing something worthwhile – and I do the cooking." She paused for a moment. "It was rough at first, but I don't think I'd trade it now for the other life." We continued in silence.

My mind tried to create a context for her remarks. Here was an attractive, young woman, living in 100 degree heat, cooking on a wood-burning stove, brushing flies out of her face with every word she spoke, walking on ground crusty with dryness, and yet, she loved it with a sincerity that was unquestionable. I wondered what the other life that she referred to must have been like, where she had come from that would make this one seem so secure.

Ian, our pilot, broke my mood. "There she is."

Below us was a fairly large homestead, and like the Bessie, only partially completed. We landed on the landing strip without incident and were greeted by the charming woman of the house, Mrs. Organ. She was not expecting visitors but was gracious and hospitable in the way Australians still are even today. No one ever seems to mind when someone drops in for a cuppa. In the Northern Territory, where distances are significant, it was tantamount to an event. Mr. Organ was away from the homestead on business.

"Hello, Holly," she smiled. "Who's this gent?" I was introduced. "Not much like New York up here, is it?"

"No, m'am," I answered. Hearing myself say those words sounded like lines from another bad movie, particularly in these rough surroundings. Next thing I expected to hear myself say was, *Are you the new school marm*?

"Come on in and have a cuppa," she said as she led us indoors. "Then you might want to have a swim over by the waterfall."

I looked in the direction she indicated but saw nothing but more of the same, which was nothing.

We had our tea in the parlor. It was nicely furnished and seemed more Victorian than Outback Australia. The furniture must have traveled quite a distance before gracing this room. Tea was served on proper china and her homemade Anzac biscuits were a new taste for me.

"Is it all right to dunk?" I asked.

"Who's this crude bastard you've brought here, Holly?" she laughed. "Go ahead, matie, dunk to your heart's content."

After tea, Mrs. Organ said, "Why don't you have a swim and I'll have some lunch for us when you get back. You know where the waterfall is, don't you Ian?"

"Righteo," Ian said.

We piled back into the plane, like jumping back into the car to drive to the store. In a few minutes we were circling a gorgeous waterfall that cascaded down into a number of pools formed by indentations in the rocks. Ian made his approach and set down a short walk from our destination.

The water was clean and lovely as it tumbled over the rock formation. Since no one had any swimming gear, I wasn't sure how to proceed. Holly kicked off her shoes and ran to the waterfall fully clothed. She stood under it, letting the water drench her from head to foot. I took off my shoes and shirt, emptied my pockets and joined her. The water was much warmer than I expected, not body temperature but not far off. It felt wonderful. Holly then leapt into one of the pools. I followed. The sun had warmed the water so much that you could bath in it.

I watched Holly frolic in the water like a child, splashing and laughing, climbing out and jumping back in. Looking at this scene somehow seemed familiar to me, as if I'd seen it all before but not exactly like this. Then it hit me. Everything in life seems to be a copy of something in Nature. Here we were in this natural swimming pool, surrounded by spectacular rock formations. I've been to hotels all around the globe that try to duplicate this very atmosphere, always falling short of the original. No wonder she was happy here.

We sat on the rocks and were completely dry in no time. As if continuing our previous conversation, she said, "Oh, I know that Jock fools around when he goes to Darwin. I wish he didn't but . . ."

There was something wistful about the way she now spoke, as if speaking for many Aussie women throughout time. She recognized there was a trade off, that her security had a price which she was willing to pay. It was so profound and at the same time so simple, so honest.

Mrs. Organ had lunch waiting when we got back to the homestead: steak, of course, fried potatoes, sauerkraut, beets and a magical custard. I was happy to find the steak considerably less work than Tom the Cook's had been. I was curious about what their life was like.

"Oh, you know," Mrs. Organ said, "we've always been Bushies. My husband and I met in the city, in Darwin. But we both grew up on stations. Can't really stand all the hustle and bustle. When we had a little money put aside, we bought this little spread and are lovin' it. We lived in more or less a tin shack before we started this homestead. Now things are a bit nicer. At least I think so."

This gave me an opportunity to say how amazed I was at the comfort their home provided.

"There is one thing that gets my dander up," she continued.

"What's that?" I asked.

"All these bloody neighbors trampin' in and out of here all the time. You can hardly get a decent day's work done."

I started to apologize for the intrusion when she clapped me on the shoulder and looked at Holly. "Tends to be a bit gullible, doesn't he? Hasn't caught on to our Aussie sense of humor yet."

We all had a good laugh, said our goodbyes and we left.

Mrs. Organ would be able to talk for some time to come about the day this humorless New Yorker came by for lunch and how he raved over her custard and swam in her waterfall and then disappeared like a breath. For his part, the New Yorker would carry the day with him as he went on to become a Californian and then a fair dinkum Aussie.

No sooner had we arrived back at the old homestead than the head stockman, Colin, came up to me.

"We wasn't introduced proper. I'm Colin," he said and extended his hand.

I took his hand and thought that if it hadn't been broad daylight, I'd have thought he put a piece of tree bark in my hand. This hand had not spent many days soaking in Ivory liquid. It was rough bordering on raspy, strong to the point of metallic. He was the very picture of a stringy, rangy cowboy. The sun had chiseled deep lines in his rawboned face. I was sure that his skin, where the sun didn't touch it, would have been as white as salt but that which was visible looked well worn. I never saw him from that moment on when he wasn't wearing jeans and a western style shirt with the sleeves rolled up to his biceps. I tried to imagine him in a suit and tie. I couldn't.

"Me an' one of the lads are goin' out for a beef. Want to tag along?"

"Sure thing," I answered.

As the truck bounced through the bush I was reminded of East Africa. Both places had a scrubby, unexplored feeling about them. There were no tracks to follow, only bits of vegetation to dodge, small poorly formed trees and shrubs. It felt to me as though at any moment a rhino could come lumbering along or an elephant. I was told there were wild animals in these parts, camels, donkeys, pigs and others, but never saw any.

We drove around for some time looking for a steer. In Africa, the hunt would have been more efficient. There would have been trackers who would examine the ground carefully for any sign: a hoof print, a tuft of hair, some spoor, a bit of blood on a thorn. This safari seemed much less scientific, much more random, where luck would have to play an essential role.

Finally a beast was sighted. Unlike its African counterpart, this animal didn't shy when he saw men approaching. It seemed totally indifferent to our presence. We got out of the truck with Colin leading the way. He had brought a small caliber rifle with him, took aim and fired a round into the steer. In Africa, one round would have brought the beast down from this distance. The rifle would have been high-powered and serious about killing what it aimed at. In this case, the steer didn't seem to notice much except that it didn't like the idea of being shot. If Colin had invested any ego in this adventure, and I suspect any man would who lived off the land like this, it would have been at least a little bit damaged by the result.

He took aim and fired another round, again hitting the steer. You could hear the smack of the bullet against his hide. Again, the steer seemed more annoyed than injured and kept traveling. I could see Colin's face flush out of the corner of my eye. I wouldn't look directly at him for fear I might laugh. He rushed into position for another shot, crouched and fired a third time. Smack! Same effect.

"Bloody bastard," Colin mumbled under his breath. He put the rifle down. "Let's get the bastard," he called to his mate.

They tore after the animal with a vengeance. While Colin tried to grab its horns and bulldog the steer to the ground, the other guy grabbed the tail and yanked it from side to side. Still no success in hauling it to the ground. Both men were sweating profusely and getting angrier by the second. The other guy then wrapped the tail around one of the steer's hind legs and while holding onto a small tree with the other hand, yanked for all he was worth. This tripped the beast and it fell. Without so much as a by-your-leave, Colin had a knife at the steer's throat and plunged it in, pulling it across and severing the jugular.

They worked together like a well-oiled machine, each knowing what needed to be done and going about his task with precision. In no time the beast was skinned and butchered. The head (sans brains), guts and hide were left on the ground. Dry leaves and branches were scattered on the truck bed to ensure cleanliness, I suppose, and the quartered carcass was loaded on. Because of the extreme heat, leaves and branches were piled on top in order to keep the meat from cooking under the blazing sun on the way back to the old homestead.

Doug and I flew back to the Bessie to spend the night. When we arrived, the men were sitting around together after their meal. A heated discussion was going on in sign language, broken English and some fair dinkum Aussie.

"You full shit. Turk best," one of the more articulate laborers shouted at Tom the Cook.

"Aw, mate, what do the bloody Turks know about bloody tobacco?" Tom the Cook replied.

"What Turk know? You bloody stupid," the laborer responded. His colleagues understood this last remark and agreed with their laughter.

Tom the Cook turned to Doug and me. "These bloody eye-ties come down here and think they know more than a bloody Aussie. Can't even talk English, bloody wogs. He says the Turks make better tobacco than we do."

"Turkish tobacco is thought of as some of the world's finest tobaccos by a lot of people," I volunteered.

Tom the Cook shot me a glance. "What are you? Another bloody expert?" He muttered as he turned away. "Bloody Yanks . . . think they know everything."

It's amazing the depth of expertise people can develop on subjects they've never had any knowledge of, exposure to or experience with. It's one of our species most endearing qualities.

I woke up next morning at half past five, having slept for more than eight hours. I was now accustomed to sleeping with the sky full of stars over my head. It felt free and natural and quite safe. I pulled on my khaki shorts and a tee shirt and joined the rest of the men at breakfast.

Tom the Cook was back to his natural good humor. Tobacco discussions seemed the farthest thing from his mind. He served us up some liver from the steer Colin had shot the day before. Chewing was not a problem this morning.

After breakfast, Doug asked me to help unload a couple of caravans from a large flatbed truck that had rolled up the night before. The heat was already intense and getting intenser. What with the heat, the dust and the resulting sweat, we had all stripped down to bare necessities and were a filthy group by the time we finished. In this condition, Tom the Cook summoned us all for tea which he served on elegant china instead of our usual mugs. Where it came from and why he chose to do it remains a mystery, but there it was.

Tom the Cook pulled his chair near to mine. "Seen any dingoes yet?"

"No, I haven't seen anything but the dogs up at the old homestead and these couple of horses that have wandered in down here."

"You know what they call a bloke that hunts dingoes for bounty?" Tom the Cook asked.

"I didn't know they hunted dingoes for bounty." I answered.

"Oh yeah, mate. They're bloody vermin around these parts." Tom the Cook said. "And the blokes that hunt them are called doggers."

"Some of them are called dog stiffeners," one of the other Aussies volunteered.

"That's right," Tom the Cook laughed. "They do call them dog stiffeners. You get that, Yank? Dog stiffeners?"

"I get it," I said.

"Yeah," Tom the Cook continued. "They take in the scalps and collect their money from the government." He paused for effect. "One bloke took in fifty-seven dingo scalps that he made out of a single calf hide he come across. He stitched 'em up real careful and let 'em dry in the sun 'til you couldn't tell what they were any more."

The other Aussie interrupted. "Wasn't that the same bloke that done the apricots?"

"Yeah, that was him," Tom the Cook agreed. "This same bloke turned a bunch of dried apricots into pig snouts – there's a bounty on them wild pigs too. Anyway, he turned these dried apricots into pig snouts by punchin' two holes in them. But the stupid bastard got caught when he got drunk one night and bragged about it to the wrong people."

"Stupid bastard," the other Aussie agreed.

"Yep. Turned apricots into pig snouts and calf hide into dingo scalps," Tom the Cook repeated. "You got to admit he was clever though."

"Stupid bastard," the other Aussie repeated.

"Stupid bastard," Tom the Cook echoed.

I decided it was time to wash off some of the dirt that was caked to my body. I headed for the shower.

"Watch that water, Yank," Tom the Cook called after me. "Let me know if it's wet enough for ya."

Doug suggested that I spend the night at the old homestead so he had Ian fly me there in time for dinner.

Without suggesting that there was any attraction, there was nevertheless an energy between Holly and me. It could have merely been that we were both relatively young and the only ones, except for Jock, in our age group. I was aware of it to some extent, but wouldn't have acted on it even if I were attracted to her. She was married. It was as simple as that for me.

However, Jock was away on this night I was to spend at the old homestead. It was natural that Holly and I spend time talking since we were the only people there, except for the ever watchful Old Col. It seemed we had a lot to talk about and we laughed a lot too. But no matter where we went or what we did, I felt the eyes of Old Col on me. He was a conscientious chaperone. It's possible that Doug asked him to keep an eye on things since it was in his best interests not to have some stranger come into his tranquil little space and make waves. Whatever the reason, there is an indelible imprint in my memory of Old Col casting sidelong glances in my direction, watching me every minute.

My bed was to be a proper bed, but not in the house where Holly slept. Mine was a wrought iron number with a high head and low foot, set up all by itself out in the yard. Even after I had bedded down under the stars in this luxurious comfort, I heard Old Col pace by, in and out of the house from time to time until the wee hours. It made me wonder who it was they didn't trust.

A little while after dawn, Holly called me in to breakfast. She had made steak and eggs for the three of us.

"And I've got something special for you," she said conspiratorially.

"What's that?" I asked.

"This," she said and brought a fresh, ripe tomato out from behind her back. "Don't you say anything, Col. He's our guest."

"Are you sure you should do this?" I asked.

"Hey, who's running this show, you or me?" she smiled.

Old Col didn't say a word, just sat there gumming his steak and slurping his eggs.

The tomato was right off the vine and tasted like the ones I used to pick from our garden when I was a kid. Nothing in the world tastes like a freshly picked, deep red tomato still warm from the sun. I was in heaven. The only thing that would have made my bliss complete would have been a glass of milk. We used goat cream in our tea that was so thick it had to be spooned out. After a few days, it lost its "goaty" taste. Only the children, naturally enough, got real milk because of its scarcity.

"I also made us a special treat," she said. "These are sort of like Australian brownies, except there's nothing brown about them 'cause there's no chocolate in them."

She put a plate of white colored cookies in front of me. They had little chunks of dried fruit in them. She poured some thick, sweet syrup over one, spooned some thick goat cream and jam on top. "Here, try this." She prepared one for Old Col and one for herself. "We love 'em, don't we Col?" He grunted his approval. You could tell that he felt very warm and protective of her. She obviously had him wrapped around her little finger.

"Have you noticed the clouds starting to build up?" she asked Old Col.

"Yep," he answered. "The Wet'll be comin' soon." These were the most words I'd ever hear him say.

Doug returned to the old homestead and in the late afternoon we all traveled down to the Bessie. As we were having tea, you could see the clouds continue their buildup. In open country like this it was quite easy to see weather roll along the horizon. In a short time, a phalanx of dust began moving in our direction in a wide swath. We could see it coming from miles away. I didn't know what it was but they all certainly did.

"We'd better get inside," Doug commanded. "Take your cakes with you."

No sooner had we huddled safely inside the several caravans than we were hit broadside by a wave of dust that lasted nearly three minutes. For those few tense minutes we were buffeted about as if under siege. When the dust passed, the air felt much cooler, suggesting that rain wasn't far behind. But it was only a suggestion.

Everything was soon packed and we were loaded onto a flatbed truck for a ride to the Bessie's waterfall. It was like being on a hayride except there was no hay.

The Bessie's waterfall was modest in comparison to Mrs. Organ's. It trickled through the crevice of some tremendous granite cliffs down into the round pool that the cliffs surrounded for about 280 of the 360 degrees. The water was pure and could be drunk as it was. It was a beautiful setting for the barbecue that Doug had decided to have in my honor.

The entire entourage was there. Head stockman Colin was there with his wife and three children. One was on her hip and the other two played in the dirt with two Aboriginal children, and some other white children, all equally crusty with dirt. Only one or two had any clothes on. Colin's wife could have been any age from twenty to fifty. She looked worn down from the life she lived in the Bush. She sprayed insect repellant into the faces of her children from time to time. But it didn't seem to make much of an impression on the flies which congregated in the corners of their eyes and around their snotty noses. It was as if the flies said, *Pfft. Yeah. Right* and went on about their dirty business.

You could see that this was a special occasion. Colin and some of the others who had wives were wearing newly laundered and ironed shirts. The ones who hadn't cleaned up ahead of time dove into the pool and came out four shades lighter.

It would have made a perfect movie set. There were logs strategically placed in an arc around a soft sandy opening that was lined around the perimeter by a few trees. The soft ground and the logs made a perfect place to sit and lean back. Beer and soft drinks were cooling in the pool while fires were set under a huge kettle of potatoes and also under a long, low slab of iron on which the meat would cook. The atmosphere was festive and a lot of joking and teasing went on amongst the men and women. Everyone gravitated toward a spot of their own while the billy boiled and soon the group was divided into families and bachelors. The laborers were especially attentive to the children and played with them. I wondered how many of them had children of their own in the Old Country. And I wondered how long it would be before they could bring them to Australia to live.

Someone had the presence of mind to bring along a transistorized phonograph. Country music seemed perfectly appropriate and we listened while Slim Dusty and others entertained us. As the moon began to rise, the insects decided to call it a day and we were left calm and peaceful in this idyllic setting.

Finally everything was cooked and served in what seemed a most efficient manner. Large slabs of bread, as big as a plate, were buttered and piled with chunks of steak and a boiled potato and sprinkled with a little salt. No plates or cutlery were necessary since it was all easily eaten by hand. Any gristle was cast into the dark where the dogs would growl over their share. A quick rinse of the hands in the pool and no worries, mate.

Les, the Aboriginal stockman, had been quite shy with me. He seemed friendly enough when we met on the first day but my contact since then had been limited. I wanted to somehow engage him in conversation. Even though his skin color was similar to that of many of my friends in New York, the cultural differences were vast and I wanted to get some notion of who this man was.

The ice was broken when he offered me his cigarette papers and some tobacco. I thanked him and looked at the fixings blankly.

"Don't you roll your own, mate?"

"I never have," I answered.

With the dexterity of a close-up magician, he flicked a bit of tobacco into the flat paper and rolled a perfect cylinder.

Colin and the others had amused expressions on their faces as Les handed the gear back to me.

I tried to duplicate his action, carefully sifting some tobacco onto the paper. When I thought I had the right amount, I put the tobacco pouch down and addressed the paper with both hands.

"It'll just roll right up now, mate. Give it a go." Les encouraged me.

I fumbled with the paper until most of the tobacco had slipped out the ends. Finally, I got it stuck together but it was nothing like the example Les had shown me. It was practically flat and so twisted up that it was mostly paper. I tried not to appear too self-conscious as I lit one end. One puff and what tobacco I had managed to keep in the paper was smoked.

"You get so you can do up a rolly on horseback with one hand," Colin said with a faint cowboy smile on his face.

"Anyone want one of these?" I asked and extended my pack of store bought cigarettes in a general direction. Practically everyone of the men took one.

Tom the Cook took a cigarette and said, "Say, Yank, you done a nice job on these. Put in a filter too." That gave them all a laugh. Predictably, Tom the Cook repeated, "Yep, even put in a filter" and flashed his two teeth in a big smile.

"I told him how we cook Galah up here," Tom the Cook said. "You ought to tell him how you Abos cook kangaroo, Les."

I looked cautiously at Les, knowing that this could be a set-up too. "How do you?" I finally asked. Even if it was going to be another joke on me, I figured it was worth it to these guys who had so little to amuse them.

"Well," Les began, "first we dig a big hole in the ground and build a fire in it. When it gets going good, we put the roo in there for two or three minutes. That burns off the hair and makes it curl up like a baby. Then we take him off the fire and gut him and put stones in the fire to heat up."

I was waiting for the "then we throw the meat away and eat the stones" but it didn't come.

"After them stones is good and hot, we put a few inside the roo's belly. Then we take the coals from the wood out and put the rest of them hot stones in the pit, put the roo on top of 'em and cover it all up with paper bark from a tree. That cooks 'em up real tender. Longer you leave it there, the better it is. Meat just falls off the bone."

"Best meat you ever put in your stomach," Tom the Cook added.

"Better than yours?" I asked. That gave everyone a good laugh and started Tom the Cook mumbling.

Someone brought a guitar out of its case and started strumming. Soon everyone was singing cowboy songs, both American and Australian. Cattlemen's voices and songs have no nationality.

The moon continued to rise and when it felt like the right time, everyone began loading up the gear and we called it a night. No announcement was made. Everyone just knew. That night was easily one of the nicest parties anyone ever threw for me.

As I lay in my cot that night, I thought about pioneers. These people were certainly pioneers in their own way. But there was a loner quality that seemed uniquely Australian. On this station, cooperation was necessary in order to do the job. But beyond these immediate surroundings, it was merely Nature that needed to be dealt with, no other hostility. There were no plains Indians whose land was being usurped. Any threat from Aboriginal Australians had been dealt with long ago with Anglo-Saxon efficiency. Australia was about a hundred years younger than the United States with a much smaller population. The backgrounds of the settlers were different too. There seems to be an innate suspicion of authority built into the Australian character based, I think, on the us-and-them relationship of jailers and convicts. So that even though people may know their nearest neighbors, each station pretty much dealt with problems on an individual basis and not a collective, communal one. Having no tangible, organized, outside threat guaranteed that.

When I woke up next morning, before I sat up, I saw that my flies were there waiting for me. I had decided that from six to twelve flies were assigned to each American tourist upon arrival in Australia. Their job was to stay as close to his face as possible throughout the day and wait patiently in a tight fly pattern above his head until morning, careful not to disturb his sleep but staying close enough to provide him a sense of security about their presence. The law required it. If they were derelict in their duties, they would be deported to New Zealand where there weren't such choice morsels available, owing to the fact that fewer Americans visited there.

It wasn't long before we got a sample of what the Wet would bring. After breakfast, the skies opened up as if someone opened a trapdoor above our heads. For about two minutes the water dumped down in one huge hunk There was no way it could soak into the ground, however much it begged for moisture. Instead, the rainwater ran off in all directions in small rivulets and disappeared. In a few seconds after it fell, the air was heavy again, muggy and uncomfortable, as if a shower had never happened.

I spent most of the day reading, looking off in the direction of the clouds from time to time, thinking I might see the rain coming. But no more precipitation was to be experienced that day. And that night I slept in my cot looking up at the stars.

Doug had another little adventure planned for me next day. He summoned Ian to fly us first to Katherine and then to Darwin. Katherine was the third largest – I hesitate to say – city in the Northern Territory, with a population of 2,000. Darwin and Mt. Isa were the largest with about 15,000 each. There were another 8,000 scattered throughout the rest of the Territory.

Doug wanted to show me an agricultural experiment that was going on in Katherine. It was called the Tipperary Land Project and consisted of a four million acre site where sorghum, rice and peanuts were being grown on land that had been unused for any agricultural purpose previously. If this experiment was successful, the claim was that it would completely change the complexion of the Northern Territory and make it a viable, contributing factor in the Australian economy.

We arrived in Darwin late in the afternoon. It was not the Darwin of today. It was pre-Cyclone Tracy Darwin. It was a far less civilized Darwin. That 1975 catastrophe had allowed a proper city to be built. To my eyes, the Darwin I saw looked like what Dodge City may have looked like to Wyatt Earp. It was low. I don't recall any buildings more than two stories high. It was weathered. The predominantly wooden buildings seemed bleached out and badly in need of paint. And it was rough. There was a frontier quality to the place that suggested anything was possible at any time. It was the nearest thing to a city for much of the Bush, where not just stockmen, but all kinds of loners and societal misfits were likely to be.

An American or European would have no concept of what dropping out in the Australian Bush is. This place felt like the end of the world, the last outpost. A much larger Aboriginal population inhabited this part of the world as well. They were generally looked down on in and around Darwin and were there principally because they couldn't live their own life style anymore and nothing else was available to them. They were thought of as lazy, shiftless, ignorant and of little value as a group. Curiously, as soon as a drop of "white" blood was mixed with theirs, all bets were off and the person was then regarded as acceptable. Many of these disenfranchised people were seen around the Welfare Offices, living off meager handouts from the government. What is it about white people, and particularly the cultural offspring of the British, that gives them such a sense of racial superiority? As if that non-pigmented skin color was somehow preferable or carried inherent advantages with it. Sometimes people really leave one scratching one's head.

Most of the people who lived in Darwin at that time were employed by the government. There was little of cultural interest. The beaches and bays and inlets looked virtually unspoiled, pristine. Swimming in the ocean was banned at the time because of sea wasps and other dangerous sea life that inhabited those waters. This made the beauty of it even more tantalizing and inviting. It could have been because I'd had too much of Tom the Cook's fare, but there were several decent restaurants in Darwin. Not *haute cuisine*, perhaps, but mighty tasty and substantial. The prices were high, however, for both food and lodging.

We checked into a small hotel, more like a motel, its principal attraction being air conditioning. Because Darwin was a place of rest and rehabilitation for many Bushies, finding a room at all was an accomplishment. Doug had phoned ahead, otherwise we may well have slept in a park as people from the south frequently did when they holidayed in Darwin during the winter months.

The pubs were naturally the center of most activities. It was said that 2 ½ pints of beer were consumed daily in Darwin for every man, woman and child. Since the women and children didn't have much of a thirst for beer, their part of the equation was meaningless. The men who kept those averages intact often used the pubs as their recreation centers as well. It was not considered unusual to observe at least one, good old-fashioned blue on any given night – or afternoon – or morning, for that matter. Mates would fight each other if no one else could be found. Then after working off some steam, would put their arms around each other's shoulders and have another beer.

Darwin had a basically shifting population. There were, however, about 6,000 Greeks who had come to Oz for a better chance at life. They were only slightly above the Aboriginals in the social hierarchy, being thought of as crude and argumentative.

Sleeping with a roof over my head felt confining. Being in this little box of a room was only acceptable when I realized that just outside its walls was the wide-open environment that I had become accustomed to over the past week or so. I didn't like the air conditioning and I didn't like the claustrophobia.

My Australian Outback adventure was coming to an end and I was supposed to return to New York and my job at the television station. The thought of going directly there with my present mindset was intolerable.

Since planes in and out of Mt. Isa only flew on certain days, I arranged for Doug to wait a few days, then wire my boss in New York and tell him that I had missed a plane and would be leaving on the next one later in the week. I also had unfinished business with Rose. I said my thank yous and goodbyes to the Bessie, the old homestead, Doug, Holly, Tom the Cook and all the rest and returned to Sydney.

Rose and I were happy to be together once again and made sure that we spent every moment together that we possibly could. I had no more plans and occupied my days with excursions she suggested around Sydney harbor while she was at work.

One day I took a boat trip to the Sydney Zoo. Since I hadn't seen any animals in the wild on my trip to the Northern Territory, I welcomed a chance to take photos of koalas and kangaroos to take back to New York for the obligatory show and tell.

Another day I cruised around Sydney Harbor and got a closer look at the Harbor Bridge and the incomplete Sydney Opera House which was the embarrassment of the day and the laughing stock of everyone who knew anything about it outside Australia.

Rose had been invited to the birthday party of an American performer who had made a huge name for himself in Australia. I'd never heard of him. His name was Don Lane. He hosted a show with a Tonight Show kind of format that featured both local and international guests. Rose had asked if she could bring me along since it was a show business event and I could be technically described as a New York television producer, even though at that time I had not yet produced any programs, only on-air promotion. I was, however, in the television industry. That much was true.

"We won't have to stay too long," she told me, "only long enough for me to say hello to a few people and show you off before I take you back to your hotel and rape you."

I was introduced to Don Lane and found him to be very standoffish. During the time we were there, I was aware of him looking my way from the other side of the room with an expression which I couldn't quite make out. He didn't seem to like me and was anything but cordial. I couldn't imagine why. The only thing I could figure out was that he resented having a New York television producer there perhaps judging him or maybe sizing him up. I don't know. But he certainly opted to reject me before I had a chance to reject him. If any of that was true, it was completely baseless. There was nothing about me that was remotely important and besides I didn't know this guy from a bar of soap. Hmm . . . maybe *that* was the problem.

The entertainment at the party impressed me a lot. It consisted of many of the guests performing for the birthday boy. I came away from it with a healthy respect for Australian talent. The culture was so isolated from the rest of the world at that time that it had developed its own Australian version of nearly everything and everyone I was already familiar with. But it all had a unique, Aussie twist that gave it a freshness that was engaging. There was something both polished and at the same time spontaneously raw about it, a "who gives a fuck" bluntness that I'd never experienced anywhere else.

I met a number of people at that party who were movers and shakers in the Australian television business. They were all cut out of the same cookie cutter as their counterparts in New York. Broadcast executives are the same everywhere. I always preferred the people who actually did things to those who told others what to do and how much money they had to do it with.

I did meet one man who characterized what I have since recognized as a unique Australian attitude. This guy was program director at a television network. As we talked about a variety of things over a beer, he told me that he was going to leave his job because he wanted to move to Queensland.

"Why Queensland?" I asked.

"I like it up there," he answered.

"Yeah, but do you have a job up there?"

"No. I'll find something to do."

"But you're a major television executive. How many jobs like that could be open?" I asked.

"I don't have to work in television," he said calmly.

To me this sounded like blasphemy. I tried to imagine anyone I knew in New York or anywhere else for that matter, in a similar position and not at least having a good prospect, if not an actual job, to go to. It was so un-American. It seemed to be so lacking in ambition, so easy and laid back. "What would you do?" I asked.

"Oh, I don't know. I'll find something. I just like the climate and the pace in Queensland better."

"You mean you'd just pull up stakes and move your family there because you like the climate? Without a job to go to?" I was still trying to get this through my head.

"Yes," he said. "I'm much more interested in the quality of my life and my family's life than any bloody job."

Perhaps he was not typical of most Aussies. Perhaps I just happened to find this one weirdo who thought that the quality of his life was of paramount importance. But he, nevertheless, became a reference point for me and I've used him time and again as a generality. The idea of it appealed to me so much that I made it an axiom of Australian life. I've since learned that there was a lot truth in it.

Rose also took me on a weekend excursion to the boarding school that her daughter attended. Rose never talked about previous relationships with me. Obviously she had either been married or intimate with somebody. She may even have had a relationship with someone going on when I arrived. The poor bastard would have been talking to himself by now, however, and probably cursing every Yank who ever set foot on Australian soil. He wouldn't have been the first. I know I would have in his place. It would have been unlikely for anyone as attractive and accomplished as Rose not to have a guy nearby, probably any one she wanted.

Her daughter was about nine-years-old, bright, freckled with her mother's red hair and creamy complexion. She was also full of fun and confident enough to be flirtatious with me. One of her friends at school, a boy, also spent the afternoon with us. He looked like he could easily be cast as Huckleberry Finn. We all had a terrific afternoon, the four of us. I learned some new Aussie words that day. I learned that "bastard" is a term of endearment when said in a particular way; I learned firsthand what "cheeky" means. Both these freckled kids were cheeky. I was also called a "dag" more than once and I must say it took a while to accept being referred to as the bits of shit stuck to a sheep's rectal wool. But eventually I did. At first glance, people think that Aussies speak a variety of British English. But it's definitely not the case. Australian English is its own species.

The concept of a boarding school was completely foreign to me. We had neighborhood schools where I grew up, which fed into the one high school. The closest to a boarding school I'd ever known of was a military school where problem boys were sent to get some discipline. The idea of living away from home during those early years seemed all too cold and detached. But these kids seemed to take it in stride, which, I suspect, is in the nature of being a kid. If it's all you know, you don't know it's unusual, no different from the number of stepparents and half siblings that are so prevalent today. Kids always seem to be able to adjust to change better than adults.

On the way back to Sydney, we traveled along country roads which cut through fields and fields of wild flowers. This natural explosion of color was as breathtaking as all the other natural wonders of this unique part of the globe. We were still about half-an-hour from the city when it began to get dark. After rehashing the afternoon one more time, Rose said, "I think I really need to feel you in me."

"You mean right now?" I asked.

"Yes. Right now."

"I don't think we can work it out in this little car," I said.

"I know," she answered and pulled the car off the road onto the dusty shoulder. "Let's get out," she said.

"Here?"

"Yes, why not? I have a blanket in the boot. We can make love under this tree." She went straight into action. In a moment, the boot was open, the blanket spread out under a huge, leafy tree and she took off her clothes. "Come on. What are you waiting for?"

After my experience in the Outback, where only the sky covered me, the naturalness of making love in the open felt completely familiar, even though I had never been naked with a woman out in nature like that before. It was so wonderfully dangerous and erotic and naughty that we lay there long after we were both spent just looking up at the starry sky and absorbing the pure thrill of it all.

As much as I wanted to put it off, I realized that this experience would have to come to an end and that I must return to New York. Rose seemed to take it in stride. Perhaps Australians have such a sense of their distance from everywhere else that these partings seem inevitable. Whatever the case, I said my sad goodbye to her and expected never to see her again, even though we promised to write.

Back in New York, after a few days to acclimate, I was back in the swing of things, telling stories about the Outback and showing slides, trying to remember Rose's face and the way she smelled and felt.

We wrote a few letters. I sent books to her daughter and her Huckleberry playmate. Some months later, Rose wrote to me that she was stopping in New York on her way to Paris. I had just begun a new relationship after my divorce and didn't want to jeopardize it. I never replied to her.

JUST SAY YES

I made two New Year's resolutions while sitting on the beach at Surfers Paradise on the Gold Coast. It was just past midnight and I needed a break from the thumping bass in the club where my friend worked as a DJ. As the waves rolled in gently and the clear sky sparkled with a million stars, I watched the steam rise from the inland area of Surfers itself. My own thoughts floated up too. First, I would make every effort to forget about a woman who had broken my heart. I would force myself to leave those things behind which could not be changed. Secondly, I would do something I had done once before, when I lived in Hollywood and things looked bleak. I would assume that nothing could come my way that was not a benefit of some kind, and would, therefore, say yes to whatever Life brought. I would trust that everything in my life was positive despite appearances to the contrary. It's not always an easy thing to do but I believe that if you can change your perception, you can change your experience. It had worked in the past. Maybe it would work again in the present.

It was after my return from the Gold Coast that a brochure arrived, sent to me by Red, a woman I knew from a production of **The Great Gatsby** that we had both been in the year before. Our contact had been limited in the intervening months and I was surprised to hear from her. The brochure announced a retreat which was to be held later in the month at a center on the Mornington Peninsula. She had attached a personal note suggesting that I might enjoy this gathering.

I remembered discussions we had had during the run of the play. Red and her parents were involved with a particular meditation discipline and traveled to different parts of the world in connection with it. I was interested in it in the way I am interested in all religion and spirituality. I've always been fascinated by the different paths people take to end up at what seems to be the same place.

When the brochure first arrived, I did my usual thing. I prepared to resist any attempt to influence my thinking and/or convince me that *this* was the right, or in some cases, only way to find happiness, equilibrium, God or whatever. While I was curious about different religions and disciplines, I was not interested in joining them, only observing their similarities.

There was a time in Hollywood when I had been curious about Buddhism. Several people I knew were involved with it and insisted that I come to a chanting meeting. One Friday evening I finally acquiesced. I found listening to the chanting of **Nom Yo Horenge Kyo** and the vibrations it set up appealing in their resonance. I didn't feel like participating but I did enjoy feeling the sound of all those voices ringing out in crisp, nasal tones. After the chanting was finished, people offered testimony of what benefits they had received during the preceding week as a result of their chanting. The enthusiasm was sort of pep rally-ish but not objectionable. If people were helped to find their way in Life by chanting, all the better. I had one friend who credits chanting with her becoming pregnant. She and her husband had been trying for years to have a child naturally. She became a Buddhist, began chanting and just before her fortieth birthday gave birth to their daughter. My attitude is: whatever works for you.

The woman who led the chanting the night I went turned to me when the testifying was finished. Perhaps because she was leading the group, she felt an obligation to push a bit harder, I don't know. In any case, she began trying to sell me. I resisted. She pressed harder. I caught myself thinking that she'd be good in a used car lot. But as a former salesman myself, I knew the tricks. I dug in more. I found it equally objectionable that any religion should need to be sold. She persisted. It became a Mexican standoff. She took a new tack.

"Can you say **Nom Yo Horenge Kyo**?" she asked.

"Of course," I answered.

"Let me hear you," she urged.

I hesitated. I didn't want this to deteriorate into a contest of wills in front of her fellow Buddhists and didn't want to be rude since I was a guest. But I also didn't want to be bullied.

"Let me hear you say **Nom Yo Horenge Kyo**," she insisted.

"Look," I said, "I have very specific spiritual beliefs which allow room for all religions but I don't necessarily subscribe to any organized discipline."

She was obviously challenged by my obstinacy and I saw her make a quick glance around at the other faces in the room. "Can't you say **Nom Yo Horenge Kyo**?"

"Of course I can say it," I answered, "I just don't choose to." She glared at me. "Look, I don't want to be rude," I continued, "but do you believe that yours is the only way to salvation or whatever it is you seek? Aren't Buddhists tolerant of other people's views?"

She ignored my question. "Why did you come here?" she asked instead.

"Because I had friends who suggested I might find it interesting or worthwhile," I answered honestly.

"And have you?"

"Yes," I said. "I find the sound of the chanting very appealing, but . . ."

"Then why can't you say the words?" she pressed.

I realized that I was boxed in. If I continued being stubborn about saying these words, I would look like a jerk. On the other hand, I didn't want to give in to her badgering. But finally I opted for the more diplomatic course and, without enthusiasm, repeated the words of the chant.

"That wasn't so difficult, was it?" she stated triumphantly.

"Not at all," I answered. "Does that make you happy now?"

Our eyes locked. Her pressure to get something, anything out of me had been relentless. What had begun as a pleasant, ecumenical experience had turned into a cheap, sales pitch. I recognized that the fundamental principles of Buddhism were like all other religions, sound and uplifting. But, in my judgment, the choice should be left to the individuals to find for themselves and not be marketed like a Big Mac or sold like encyclopedias. I was so offended by the woman's tactics that I lumped Buddhism in with her zeal and discarded them both until I learned better from other people. It appears that I was not the only one offended by these tactics. A couple of years later, I was informed that the Buddhist leaders in Japan condemned that kind of behavior, were embarrassed by it and insisted that it stop. It had been mainly an American, or perhaps, Southern Californian aberration. Angelinos wanted to be the biggest, best and baddest Buddhists in the world.

With that as background, I was cautious about any religion or religious experience. I telephoned Red and thanked her for sending me the brochure.

"I think you'll really enjoy this," she said. "It's going to include artists from around the world who are coming for this event."

"What kind of artists?" I asked.

"All kinds. There are some from Italy and South America. Lots of different places. Dancers, actors. After the conversations we had during the play, I thought this might be a chance for you to see what I was talking about." Her demeanor was light and it sounded as though she really thought I might enjoy it. Then she added, "It doesn't cost anything, only whatever you want to pay at the end."

"What?" The very openness of it left me in shock.

"Yeah, you don't have to bring anything except what the brochure says, an instrument if you play one and that's it. Food, blankets, pillows, all that stuff is provided."

"When do I have to let you know?" I asked.

"I'm pretty sure you can still get in at the last minute, but tell me as soon as you decide one way or another."

I promised I would.

Later that day I was visiting my friend, Sally. She had also been in **The Great Gatsby** with Red and me. I told her of my conversation with Red and showed her the brochure.

"I think I'd be keen to do this," Sally said.

"You would?"

"Yeah, it could be interesting."

While I was re-thinking my initial reluctance, I remembered my New Year's resolution. "I'm going to do it." I announced.

"Maybe I will too," Sally added.

* * *

We found ourselves on a train going south on the evening the retreat was to begin. Everyone was to arrive by dinnertime. We were going to be a little late but I had called ahead and asked that they save some food for us. I was assured that it would be no problem. As we listened to the wheels clack along the track, we tried to imagine what we had gotten ourselves into.

"If we don't like it, we can always leave early," I suggested.

"I wonder what it's going to be," she mused.

"An adventure," I answered.

The women at the reception desk were dressed in white. Their friendly manner was reassuring. I had expected to have a room to myself because I had been granted permission to bring along my pet bird. Therefore, I was surprised to learn that I had been put in a room with a German man. Since I hadn't brought the bird, it didn't matter.

At the designated time, we were all summoned to the White Room, a large meeting room which would be our headquarters for group gatherings. It was a rectangular room with chairs arranged around its perimeter. Several pillows were scattered on the floor in the middle of the room. When I got there, all the chairs were occupied and people were already seated on the pillows. I spotted a doorway inside the room which led to a large closet. I leaned against the doorframe and thereby had a strategic position from which to observe everything.

A friendly woman named Maddy, originally from Holland, was the organizer of the retreat and assumed the duties of chairing the gathering. She introduced herself and asked that we in turn introduce ourselves and specify in what area of the arts our interests lay.

Beta, the German who was to be my roommate, sat next to Maddy. It was clear from the very beginning that he was clever, confident and fluent in English. He began talking about his style of dance as "kitchen sink" art because it incorporated everything but that particular item. He had come to this retreat from Berlin.

Each person identified themselves. By the time the nearly fifty of us had gone through this exercise, we learned that there were dancers, actors, mimes, presenters, singers and musicians from Russia, Argentina, Ukraine, Peru, Germany, Holland, Kenya, India, Italy, Australia and the United States. if I was counted as being from my country of origin. Many, but not all, now lived in Australia. If America is a melting pot, Australia is at least a melting sauce pan.

Maddy gave us some idea of what we could expect for the next five days We were expected to wear indoor shoes indoors and outdoor shoes outdoors There was to be no smoking anywhere in the building. We would start each day with some kind of physical exercise, have a meditation session before breakfast and most afternoons would be free. We were asked to be quiet when we were in the sleeping section of the building and put cups and plates, etc. in the kitchen when we were finished with them. We were told that the days would begin early so we might want to go to bed at a reasonable hour.

All the food was vegetarian and prepared by volunteers who meditated over it for good measure.

"For those of us who have not yet found our way onto your clock," I asked, "is there someplace where we can congregate until we get sleepy?" I seemed to have struck a common chord as many heads bobbed.

After a brief consultation with the White Lady, Maddy told us we could hang out in the dining room as long as we were respectful of others' desire to sleep and kept the noise down. When the introductory meeting ended, several of us made a beeline for the dining room. Beta, an actress I'll call Sydney, Sally, and a couple of other people were sitting at a table, drinking coffee when I joined them.

There was an eagerness to get to know one another from the beginning. This led me to ask what brought people to this retreat. Beta, like myself, had said, "Why not?" and trekked around the world to Australia to check it out. Others seemed to be searching for something specific in their lives and were willing to pursue any avenue to try to find it. Some had attended a similar gathering in India the year before which was sponsored by this same group. Some were attracted by the arts aspect. The reasons for being there were as varied as the participants.

When it came time to hit the sack, Beta and I walked quietly to our room. Once we shut the door, we began talking like guys who'd known each other for a lifetime. We talked about the women at the retreat, of course. Then we talked philosophy, or more accurately, spirituality.

Then the subject of Butoh, the kind of dancing he did, came up. I had never heard of it before. To me, the gist of it was that Butoh is more than just a kind of dance. It approaches a life style, a sense of freedom that is largely improvisational and very much in the moment. If I were describing it in a Hollywood pitch session, I'd say it was Sixties Love Children Meet Isadora Duncan in Berlin in the 1920s. There was a feeling of total abandon with a pinch of decadence about it. From looking at Beta, it was easy to assume that it didn't require the same kind of physical discipline as ballet.

He didn't look like any dancer I'd ever seen. His head was shaved and his chest was concave. He wasn't particularly muscular and his wire-rimmed glasses and cadaverously thin face gave him the appearance of a mad scientist. He had a wide, toothy smile and laughed easily.

We found so much common ground instantly that we could have kept talking all night. But good judgment got the better of us. We finally talked ourselves out and the light went off.

I lay in the dark, attempting to put the events of the day in perspective. It was as though I was in a foreign land, away from everything familiar. The transition was instantaneous. No long trip had eased me into this new situation. It was more like time travel. One minute I was in Melbourne, the next in Xanadu or Shangri-La. I opened the window and listened to the wind in the trees for a while. Then all was silent . . . except for Beta's steady breathing.

* * *

His alarm went off about ten minutes before our exercise session was to start. We hustled ourselves to an outdoor circle which was called The Circle and got our *chi* flowing. The exercises were simple and I made a mental note that only about half the people were there.

We took our now pumping *chi* into the White Room where the White Lady presided. She was the main religious leader at this center, a very soft-spoken, articulate woman with a lovely, calm demeanor and a childlike laugh. She would lead us through our morning meditation sessions and explain the discipline that these people followed. I found her message to be **THE** message of a Higher Being and our relationship to it. Only in this case, the White Lady identified the Higher Being mostly as He, sometimes She, but definitely in the form of a person. I personally have no problem with this. People often get hung up on the semantics of spirituality and ignore the fact that the principles are virtually the same. This seems silly to me. So after her introduction and explanation of the technique used in this discipline, I felt that it was something I could do without compromising any of my own principles and, therefore, entered into the meditation without prejudice. That is until one of the regulars began leading the actual meditation.

While the meditation, itself, didn't offend me, the fact that someone was going to lead my mind through it did. You can't have lived in Southern California for as long as I did without hearing someone lead a meditation of some sort, accompanied by new age music. I personally prefer the tranquility without help. But I gritted my teeth and used the time to look around the room at the faces. To my pleasant astonishment, they were uniformly peaceful. My natural cynicism began to evaporate. There was obviously nothing threatening or even demanding about this exercise.

It turns out that a number of the people in attendance had been not only following this discipline for quite some time, some actually lived at this center as a refuge until they were able to face the world again. This aspect of the place impressed me greatly. It was a place where someone who wasn't coping very well could drop out and get it together without having to pay for their keep, just work it off by doing chores around the building and grounds. Everyone benefited. Then when the time was right, it would be back to the real world, no questions asked.

The first formal session was held in a room that was set up as a kind of cabaret. There were a number of round tables placed around a large room which also had a small stage at one end. About ten chairs were at each table. It became our cafe. I tried to avoid sitting with anyone I knew. The procedure was that each table would discuss a common topic which was displayed as the Menu of the Day. The topic was quite esoteric and general enough to allow nearly anything to fit into it. This day's topic was "PASSION - WHAT IS MY MOTIVATION OR DRIVE TO PERFORM & CREATE? WHY HAVE I CHOSEN TO BE AN ARTIST?"

My first reaction to this was predictably negative. I have a problem referring to myself as any kind of artist. The word catches in my throat if I'm talking about myself. I, therefore, think it is presumptuous for people to refer to themselves as an artist. Unless the world has made this determination, it seems a bit egotistical to me. But as people began approaching the subject, it became clear that I was the only one who had a problem. So I loosened up and listened to what was being said.

A lovely Irish man, Jigs, with his beautifully lilting accent, personalized the topic and recounted his experience as an itinerant musician. "Music is all I've ever wanted to do," he explained. "And mostly jazz. There's nothin' like gettin' together with some other musos and jammin'." His eyes got misty. "I never thought I'd be so lucky as to make a livin' doin' somethin' that meant so much to me. But, wouldn't you know – a job came up at this school where they were looking for someone to teach music. Me wife encouraged me to try for it and I've been there ever since, twenty-one years. The students and me even have a little jazz combo." He had no problem thinking of himself as an artist.

Others at the table had similar experiences to share. I was embarrassed at my earlier cynicism and reminded myself that I had done all this voluntarily and it wasn't my place to sit in judgment of anyone. Finally, as the session wound down, I got out the Green Book.

The Green Book is my own invention. Some time ago, when I was living in New York, for reasons I can't recall, I began copying things I'd come across into this three-ring, green plastic covered binder. The inclusions varied from things that had to do specifically with acting to performing in general to philosophy and then anything that resonated at any particular time. My method in gathering this material was random. Over time, I found that I had assembled a lot of quotes from a lot of sources which, taken all together, had something for virtually any situation. I had decided to take the Green Book with me to the retreat. Something told me that it might be useful.

My contribution to the discussion at our table was a quote from the Green Book by Oliver Wendell Holmes, Jr., Chief Justice of the United States Supreme Court. The quote was: ***"If I were dying, my last words would be, Have faith and pursue the unknown end."*** It seemed to strike a chord among the people at our table and at the conclusion of the session, I was asked to share it with the entire group. The Green Book became a part of the retreat experience from that moment on.

At lunch I singled out Lydia to talk to. She was a sports presenter for a Kenya television station in Nairobi and seemed quite reserved. She was one of those who had attended a similar retreat in India the previous year.

Because she looked in a general way like African American women I had known in the States, I assumed I had more in common with her culturally than I actually did. Unlike women I'd known, however, Lydia was from a country whose population is predominantly Black and had been for her entire life; whose government is Black and had been for her entire life, and whose culture is not an amalgamation where she was just another flavor, but genuinely African and had been for her entire life. African Americans know that even though they were born on American soil and their ancestors had shed their blood in every American war, their status was always subject to question. I've had conversations with African Americans who now live in

Australia. Every one of them comments on the enormous difference and sense of self they have in a country which doesn't carry that particular racial stigma. One even said, "I'd like all my friends back in the States to spend one day in Australia so they could see what it feels like to just be yourself."

After lunch, the early afternoon was ours to do with whatever we chose. I decided to take a walk outside the grounds to find a pay phone and check my messages. I left the grounds and wandered along the road in the direction I thought would lead me to a Shell station I'd seen on the way in. After some trial and error, mostly error, I found one. I was reminded of when I was a traveling salesman.

After college and the Army, I got a job on the road selling. As a traveling salesman, it would be useful to have a good sense of direction. However, my boss, who lived in a suburb of Chicago, always had one of my colleagues meet me at my hotel and lead me to the boss' home whenever we had meetings there. His theory was that arty guys always get lost. In his eyes, I was an arty guy. In a way he was right. I did get lost. I always try to allow myself extra time when going somewhere new for that reason.

I found the Shell station and walked in.

"Do you have a pay phone?" I asked.

"Naw, mate. Sorry." I started to walk away. "Where do you want to call?"

"I just want to call my phone in Melbourne and check messages."

"You won't be long, will ya, mate?" he asked.

"No. Just long enough to see if anyone called," I answered.

"Here, use this one," he said and pulled his business phone from behind the counter. The problem was that it didn't have the tone necessary to activate my message machine. I explained the problem to him.

"Look, mate, there's a little group of shops just up the road there. I think there's a phone box there," he said. He pointed me in the right direction and off I went.

I finally found the shops and there was indeed a pay phone in front of one of them. It had the necessary tone to activate my machine. That is to say, it would have if it had been in service. But it wasn't. I walked back toward the retreat center. There was another moment of uncertainty when I reached a fork in the road. I hadn't paid attention when going in the other direction and wasn't sure which way to go. I made a choice, realized after fifteen minutes or so that it had been the wrong one, backtracked and eventually found my way back to the center.

At the reception desk, I explained my dilemma to the women there and they asked if I'd like to use their phone. I hadn't wanted to ask before because I didn't think it was proper. Under these circumstances, however, I reconsidered my initial reluctance and called my machine. At the appointed time, I pressed the keys to activate the messages. This phone didn't have the required tone either. I decided that it was the Universe's way of telling me to forget about the rest of the world and be just where I was. I didn't try to call after that.

I heard some cool sounds coming from what I'll call the music area. There was a piano and a variety of percussion instruments located on a sunken level between the dining room and the reception. A number of couches and comfortable chairs also decorated the rather large space. The cool sounds came from someone playing jazz on a soprano sax accompanied by piano and guitar. The sax was being played by Jigs, the Irishman. I was attracted to this music and felt an urge to contribute.

There were a couple of African drums sitting around unused which I put together and held in place between my knees, turning them into makeshift bongos. I picked up the rhythm and laid down a groove. For a while we made beautiful music. But it soon deteriorated because all three of the other players decided that they'd solo at the same time and it became chaos. Just when we were beginning to get our groove back, we were told that the schedule demanded we move on to the next thing, sculpting with clay on the verandah outside the music area. True to my nature, my back automatically went up. I have always hated being told what to do, especially when I'm having fun. But I kept it to myself and walked onto the verandah.

Many people had already picked up blocks of clay and were doing their thing. Despite what my sales boss said about my being arty, I have never had any talent with fine art, whether it be painting or sculpting. I never played with clay as a kid and staying within the lines of a coloring book was as close as I came to the other art form. I went from table to table, observing everyone's talent, thus prolonging the time before I made my own leap into this artistic abyss. I was procrastinating nicely; happy to appreciate the obvious and considerable talents of the others, until Sally dropped a block of the milk chocolate colored stuff in my hand and said, "Make something."

I put the rectangular prism of clay on the table in front of me and announced that it was a loaf of freshly baked bread. From across the verandah, Sally gave me a look that needed no further explanation. So I pulled some of the clay off the block and began rolling it around in my hand, making it into a sphere, something for which I was sufficiently talented. After I had one ball of clay as close to perfect as possible, I tore off another piece from the block and rolled it into another, smaller ball. Before long I had four balls of varying sizes. I could have gone on making these perfect little spheres indefinitely, but like every artist, I needed a new challenge, something to stretch my skills and imagination. What would it be? Aha! I put one ball on top of another and decided that they were the beginning of something. I studied my creation and waited for it to speak to me. Soon, it was saying in a high pitched voice, "Come on, Pluto." That's it! Mickey Mouse in 3-D. I flattened the two smaller balls and stuck them on as his ears, made a little snout with a tiny ball on the end and finally added a tail. From the back, looking over Mickey's shoulder, it wasn't a bad likeness. The big ears were the key. As the *piece de resistance* I rolled three or four itsy-bitsy balls and placed them at his rear, next to his tail. They looked like little turds and completed my artwork perfectly.

The people who bothered to look at my creation made a tolerant little nod and went on about their own artistic business. I looked around for someone who would really be able to appreciate primitive, folk art and spotted Beta at another table. His block of clay was untouched in front of him.

"What are you making?" I asked as I approached him.

"I am still thinking," he answered. "What haf you done?"

I showed him my 3-D Mickey Mouse and got the desired response from him. He laughed.

"I like ze little shits zat you haf in ze beck," he said in his wonderfully German accent. I realized that Beta was the only one with sufficient sensitivity to appreciate real art and decided to help him discover his own masterpiece.

"That looks like a loaf of freshly baked bread," I told him, hoping that Sally wouldn't hear me.

I rolled a little hunk of clay into a small ball, something which, in all modesty, I had mastered by now. "And this is a truffle," I said as I handed it to him.

He took the "truffle" from my hand and examined it closely. "Ya, I see ze pozzibilities now." He found a small twig on the ground and stuck the "truffle" on the end of it. "But zis is not a truffle," he said. "It is a cherry." He placed the "cherry" on the stick and plunged it into the loaf of freshly baked bread. "Zis artistic creation is now called 'Cherry Brot.'"

We began waxing poetic about our contributions to the world of sculpture, amusing ourselves no end, until others also saw the value of our art. Before long, several people had joined in the spirit and we had moment after moment of, literally, sidesplitting laughter. It was all so stupid that it eventually had to be funny. That afternoon was the beginning of the pure, hearty, raucous laughter which characterized the rest of our time together. It became the cleansing agent for everyone who was around us from that moment on.

Once again I had proven to myself not to prejudge a situation and just go along. I had grumbled to myself about giving up a wonderfully spontaneous musical moment against my will and found myself having the best laugh I'd had in months. "Remember," I told myself, "you're saying yes to everything."

* * *

Later in the afternoon we were to have another meditation session. This time we were in a different, quiet room. Chairs were arranged to focus on a wall which was virtually a screen. There were three candles on the floor in front of the screen, a taller one in the center and two shorter ones on either side. In the center of the screen was a single pinpoint of light. That pinpoint of light was to be our focus for the meditation. There was soft, new age type music playing as we entered and seated ourselves. The setting was tranquil and lovely.

I found myself enjoying this moment of serenity and began easing my way deeper into it when my illusion was shattered once again by someone wanting to lead me through her meditational experience rather than allowing me to enjoy mine.

But again, my better judgment kept my lips sealed. Instead I looked around the room at the others and discovered that they appeared to be enjoying this vocal assistance. I felt like a square peg in a round hole.

We had a special treat for dinner that evening. The food people had set up their galley out in the open, near a dam. Benches were arranged around a stack of firewood. Some people had brought blankets to spread around on the ground close to the would-be fire. To my utter astonishment, one of the volunteers walked up to the wood and poured petrol all over the top of it, struck a match and up it "whooshed" into a brilliant flame . . . for about thirty seconds, until the petrol had burned off, leaving the perfectly stacked wood virtually intact, not even charred. There had been no paper or kindling or any kind of starter placed at the bottom of the woodpile. As someone who is constitutionally incapable of leaving a fire alone, I got up and started pushing some twigs under the stack of wood. Others brought paper and other bits of wood. Before long we had a proper fire crackling.

Because of my obsession, I kept an eye on the fire, prepared to add wood and adjust as needed. As I glanced at the faces around the fire, I spotted Sara, who'd engaged me in conversation when I first arrived. She also had her eye on the fire. At the perfect moment, a split second before I was about to make my own move, she leapt to her feet, went "bap, bap, bap," tossed a couple of new pieces of wood on and had the fire blazing. It was so expert and confident and efficient that I just sat in total awe. I had misjudged this woman entirely. I had thought she was just another pretty face. Instead, she was a descendant of the Great Fire God.

The wind kicked up every now and then, throwing showers of dancing sparks all around. They represented no real danger because most of them cooled before landing on anyone and if they did, were brushed away without harm. But the effect was impressive pyrotechnics. Whenever the wind gusted, spark spirits swirled heavenward, filling the darkness for a moment with a lively show. But on the down side, the gusting wind also tended to blow a lot of smoke around. This was not as pleasant as looking at the dancing sparks. There was no way to avoid it as long as one stayed out there. The warmth of the fire was coveted by all and a functional proximity guaranteed smoke in the face. It was a trade off most people accepted, even though next morning many had bloodshot eyes and that night's clothing held the aroma of burning wood for days.

After we'd had our food, there was a kind of self-conscious silence that descended. Little pockets of conversation were evident but nothing that included the group as a whole. Maddy was prepared for this lull and took the floor. She wanted us to share some high moments in our lives, something which had a spiritual connotation. A few people told of experiences they'd had which loosely qualified.

When another lull was approaching, a woman's voice said, "I would like this group to tell me what I'm doing wrong. I'm a really good actor and I want to know why I'm not more successful."

Now there's a question, I thought to myself. What she expected to hear or learn from a bunch of strangers about success in her chosen field was a mystery to me.

"People have been programmed," she continued, "to keep me from doing what I do. How can I get them to take me seriously? I'm really good at what I do," she insisted.

I was amazed at the compassion which followed as people actually tried to help this woman, suggesting ways to overcome her obstacle.

I had brought the Green Book with me to the campfire. People were interested to see if there was anything in it to fit this situation. I looked through it and found a quote which I'd taken from a Christian Science pamphlet. It said, **". . . be what we want the world to be like."** Her response was to say, "yes, but . . ." As soon as you get a "yes, but . . ." you know that whatever you said didn't take. To my eternal gratitude, Maddy decided to move the discussion on.

Other people returned to the original subject and shared moments of personal epiphany. A well-known music theatre performer told about a song which was always requested of her when she sang at an annual Christmas celebration. This song was very simple, she told us, but had something magical about it and no matter how often she sang it, it had the same effect both on her and her audience. Obviously, once she mentioned it, there was no way she would be allowed to avoid singing the song for us. She did an a cappella version which was absolutely lovely and everyone around the fire understood why her audiences demanded it.

Something in the air, maybe the sparks or maybe the magic of the song, whatever it was brought Lydia, the reticent African, to life. Suddenly, she was alive and out of her shell in an instant. She became flirtatious and cute with the entire assembly and took center stage as if she were doing her own performance art. There was a song which she insisted on singing. She also demanded a guitar and one was provided. It was of little use, however, as she couldn't play it herself. After a moment or two to discover this, without relinquishing the stage, she finally launched into the song. It turns out that others also knew this song and joined in with her. It was a limited community sing but it, in turn, sparked others, no pun intended, into action.

A man whom I'll call Falsetto then performed an original composition, accompanying himself on the guitar which Lydia couldn't play. The song was good but his singing was heavenly. It became more and more obvious that there was a great deal of talent amongst us.

Another woman, who had come from Holland to attend the retreat, decided to share an experience with us:

"I don't know why I tell you dis story. But maybe you understand me better. I vas in Amsterdam, still an ector, with much theatre shows I haf done. I vas vorking in a play with a famous Polish director. Maybe you know. Stanislaus Marcek. He is wery famous in Holland. And he does wery *avante guarde* things, sometimes with no talking, only activities and so. My part in dis play vas for folding sheets. He want me to fold sheets in de play. I fold sheets every day of rehearsals for four months. Only folding sheets. I don't haf vords or what you call speeches, only folding de sheets. But he don't like de vay I fold de sheets even dough I practice for many hours each days. I try and try to please de maestro but he don't like my folding. I vas really trying to do dis correct but he thinks I am not so good. On de day we open and we have rehearsal in de afternoon, Maestro says me he going to cut my folding of sheets. 'But I haf den nothing to do on stage,' I tell him. 'I am vorking and vorking so hard on de folding all dis time.' But he says me dat the folding is not good and we must drop from de play. 'But what do I do?' I ask him. He says me dat he vants me in kitchen."

Everyone thought, as I did, that she meant that there was a kitchen area on the set where she would be instead of wherever she was folding sheets. But no. "I tell him **kitchen**! You vant me in kitchen? He says me yes. And I say 'What I am doing in kitchen?' And he says me to cook for cast and keep kitchen clean. So I am not being in play anymore after much months of folding of sheets, only in kitchen."

We couldn't help laughing. If she had intended it to be a comedy routine, she couldn't have done it better. She accepted our reaction good-naturedly. Then she capped it with an unintended punch line. "I am still loving acting but now I am personal manager for other actors and don't go on de stage no more."

* * *

Next day, after a quick shower, we headed out to The Circle for our morning gym class. Mimi, let's call her, a mime from Argentina had decided she would lead the exercises this morning. She was an interesting person to have at this retreat. She spoke no English, some French and lots of Spanish, thus limiting the number of people she could converse with. She guided us through some loosening up exercises and in some magical way, we all felt connected to this woman even though most of us couldn't understand a word she said, nor could she understand us.

At the morning meditation, the White Lady got a little more specific about her religious practice. While she was elucidating, there came a moment when she had to refer to God once again. By now it was clear that when she used this word, she meant it as a person, or if not that, at least a personality. She asked for a show of hands. Who believed in God?

I sort of halfway made a motion with my hand, as noncommittal as I could make it. I would really like to have been able to qualify what I meant by God before committing myself one way or the other. Beta, on the other hand, didn't have trouble responding. His hand remained in his lap. White Lady had an eagle eye and pounced on Beta as if he'd been a trout in her favorite stream.

"You don't believe in God?" she asked him pointedly.

"Well, I believe in somesing," he said, "ozerwise ve would not exist. But I don't think zere is some man up zere with a long beard on cloud number seven who tells me what to do and what I should not do."

White Lady had also noticed my reticence. "And you?" she asked.

"Yes," I said.

"Yes, what?" Everyone laughed.

"Yes . . . what he said." It also got a laugh from everyone but White Lady. She was serious without being stern. "I mean I believe in a Life Force," I continued. "Without it I wouldn't be here. And maybe without me, it wouldn't be here either. I don't know. But I think we are all a part of this continuous river called Life. You can call it God or Supreme Consciousness or whatever you want, but there's no denying that it is." I couldn't tell what White Lady was thinking. She just looked at me with her peaceful, tolerant eyes for a second longer. Then she aimed them toward the back of the room.

"And what about you?" she said, looking at the Fire Goddess, Sara.

Without missing a beat, as if she'd been ready for this one, she started. "Actually, I have trouble with the word God." There was militancy in her voice. This was obviously not the first time she'd dealt with the subject.

White Lady quickly returned to her talk, leaving Sara's militancy hanging there like cloud vapor. "Our meditation can help you in many ways in dealing with anger, frustration, disappointment and other problems that we all have in Life. There are more than 500,000 people who practice this form of yoga in seventy-five countries around the world. We could not have grown so large if there was not something to it."

Half-a-million people out of the world's population didn't seem all that impressive to me, particularly coming from Southern California where there was a different kind of spiritual discipline in every canyon, each of which could have fielded a pretty substantial team. But White Lady's perspective was different from mine. I wasn't a woman from India who would have been treated like a princess until she got married and a slave thereafter. She was. She had been handpicked by the founder to do this work. It gave her a stature and position of respect which she might not otherwise have experienced in her life. To her the work was necessary and the numbers meaningful.

"Now we will have ten minutes of meditation," she announced. A mask of peace came over her face instantaneously. The same guy who poured petrol on the fire the night before started the tape player and soothing, new age music filled the room. People settled into themselves and a calm ensued. I was settling into it nicely when the Fire Guy began leading the meditation.

Here we go again, I thought to myself and braced my consciousness for the onslaught of words which I knew was to follow. True to my prediction, Fire Guy told us how he was leaving his body and becoming a pinpoint of light, a light I would happily have seen burning less brightly, by the way. Then, he said, he approached the light and became one with the light and ran into someone else he recognized. How you can recognize one pinpoint of light from another was a concept I couldn't grasp, but never mind. Then this other light recognized him and they apparently had a nice long jawing session because this went on for at least twenty minutes, including three false endings. He was a veritable Beethoven the way he would lead me to think it was over, only to stretch it out a bit longer. I was exhausted when he finally finished and promised myself that I'd think twice about attending any more of these sessions. They may have been beneficial to others, of which I had no doubt. But for me it was a Sam Goldwyn: *include me out.*

At breakfast that morning, I sat at a table with Beta and three Russian women. The youngest, Naya, was a nineteen-year-old violinist. She seemed to be mature beyond her years in many ways and very much a girl in others. Probably because she was away from any kind of parental supervision, she felt completely free to do as she chose. Her flashing brown eyes gave life to the Russian folk song; "Ochi Tchorniye" Beta got most of her attention. She also had those dark eyes focused on a career as a concert violinist and was conscientious about practicing every day we were there. Another of the Russians played the piano. Anna was a woman of indeterminate years, somewhere in her thirties or forties, very cautious and quiet, but always there. The third, Tanya, was a dancer. She had been trained as a ballerina in Russia. She told us she was born on the Russia-China border in a train. She had a natural curiosity about things occult and spiritually offbeat.

As we sat in the dining room at breakfast, looking out the large windows at the colorful Rosella's feeding in the trees, the laughter we generated was almost embarrassing. People at other tables couldn't ignore us and often looked over after one of our outbursts with smiles on their faces which seemed to ask what could possibly be so funny, as if they wanted to be infected by this contagion themselves. The Rosella's led us to a discussion of nature in general which led into a discussion of human nature in particular, a subject which meandered around sex without landing on it until Tanya got specific.

In her beautifully Russian accent, she asked, rhetorically, "Why is not sex spoken of with this group?" She wasn't being provocative. It was merely a matter of curiosity. "You know these white ladies practice celibacy," she answered herself. She had previously attended similar events at this retreat center and was more knowledgeable than any of the rest of us.

"Well, zen, I beliefe we haf an obligation to talk about zese sings," Beta replied. "None of us would be here wizout such prectices," he added with a big smile.

It opened the subject of men and women which Beta and I had been discussing and laughing about in all our private conversations. Like most men I've ever known, we were mystified by the inability of men and women to really understand and, therefore, communicate on a completely honest level with one another. The desire for contact is undeniable but all attempts to live together and especially understand one another was a useless exercise, doomed to failure.

Like most women I've ever known, the three Russians took the position that men and women could, in fact, live together happily in complete understanding if men were open to expressing their feelings and communicating with their partners.

"Zis is exactly ze point," Beta said. "By being naturally ourselfes, ve cannot reach zis understanding. It is only if men change zat we can be perfect mates to a woman. Zis is impozzible. You don't ask zese birds to change. We are alzo animals zat cannot change."

"But we want you to treat us as equals," Naya demanded.

"We are not equal," Beta replied. "Women haf all ze power already. Men are just there to service them. Women control everysing with their sexual parts, with ze pussy."

It was wonderful having this discussion in English. It meant that people had to use the words available in their vocabulary instead of euphemisms. Obviously, Beta's English vocabulary had been forged in colloquial surroundings. I have often credited this as the British Empire's most meaningful contribution to the world, viz., the English language. Even though it lands on the ear differently depending on where one is from, it still provides us with a foundation for global communication. In my opinion, it comes close to balancing the British Empire's other major social contributions to the world: racism, arrogance and bigotry . . . and capitalism.

This breakfast discussion seemed to set the tone. It may have been because we were all in this place together. It may have been because of some vibration which was set up by the center. It may have been for reasons that are inexplicable. But there was a kind of unrestricted openness and candor and trust which permeated the atmosphere of the retreat that morning which gave us all permission to say what we liked without fear of judgment or criticism.

At that morning's cafe session, I located myself at a table where a few people were already seated, Jigs, the Irishman, being the only one I had known previously. Naya and Beta joined me and soon after that Sara, the Fire Goddess. An Indian classical dancer from Mumbai named Sushi joined us. I had had no contact with her up to this point. She was very retiring and shy to the extent that she seemed almost unapproachable. Her face was lively and animated when she spoke but the rest of the time it was very neutral and reserved. The final chair was taken by the woman from the night before who wanted us to tell her why she wasn't successful as an actor.

Our subject this day was "DREAMING - WHERE DO CREATIVITY & INSPIRATION COME FROM? WHAT IS THE SEED OF CREATION." Sara, the Fire Goddess, chaired our group with the same authority she'd tended the fire. She was very strict about keeping the discussion moving and prevented any prolonged personal concerns from taking hold, especially by the WHY woman who used every opportunity to pull the discussion back to her torment. I found something in the Green Book which I thought might help. It was a quote from "The Alchemist" by Paulo Coelho: ***"There is only one thing that makes a dream impossible to achieve: the fear of failure."*** It did nothing to relieve the woman's suffering. Then I pulled another one out: ***"You are not a failure until you stop trying."*** It became a self-fulfilling prophecy. I stopped trying to help her.

When this session was about to conclude, Maddy informed us that we were to spend the afternoon, until meditation time, in complete silence.

I knew I couldn't trust myself during the silent period so I left the grounds after lunch and walked to the Shell station for an ice cream. This time I was sure of my way and found it with no detours. How many days had we been in this place? How many more were there to go? Time seemed to have become irrelevant. The intensity of the experience itself had overshadowed it.

I began to feel embarrassed again at my attitude toward the silent period. It's so easy to criticize. I realized what a hypocrite I was, on the one hand relishing this opportunity to commune with the world, as it were, and on the other bitching to myself about how this communion was brought about and manifested. As I walked along in the warm sunlight, crunching the chocolate coating on my ice cream, I remembered what had brought me here in the first place. By the time I returned to the retreat center my frame of mind and attitude were much improved.

I strolled around the considerable grounds, content to talk to the trees. I found the track which led to where we'd congregated around the fire and strolled along it aimlessly. Soon that track led to another which seemed to skirt the entire perimeter of the grounds. As I ambled along in that direction I thought I heard footsteps. I stopped and listened, then moved in their direction. In a moment, two of the Russians women, Tanya and Anna, came into view. They were speaking softly in their native tongue. When they saw me, I nodded. They returned my nod and then asked me where I'd been.

"I just took a little walk off the grounds," I answered. "Where is everyone else?"

"Many people decided to take a nap," Tanya informed me. "That way they don't need to worry about talking."

"Naya and Beta are here somewhere," Anna motioned. "She has to practice so he made her play for us. It was lovely."

See, I said to myself, *look what you've missed by being a rebel.*

We walked along together back toward the buildings and when we came to a clearing near one of the rear entrances, there were Beta and Naya. That evening's schedule called for a performance night during which people would have a chance to show others their work. None of the five of us had given any thought to what we would do. As we sat on the grass together, I floated a trial balloon.

"Why don't we do something together?"

"Like what?" Tanya asked.

"Well, I brought my baritone ukulele with me and I can play a Russian folk song. I even think I know the words," I said.

"Which song is that?" Anna asked.

"I don't know what it's called in Russian. I just learned it from a record my sister had. It goes like this." I sang, in what turned out to be understandable Russian, a song I'd learned from a Paul Robeson recording. The three Russians all knew the song, of course.

"We can play it . . ." Naya said, indicating herself, Anna and me.

"And ve can dense to it," Beta added, indicating Tanya and himself.

We decided to call ourselves Russian Passion.

After dinner, everyone assembled in the big room where we held our cafe sessions. The tables had been cleared away leaving the entire space open. Chairs were arranged around the perimeter of the room on each of which were draped several pieces of cloth. Those who had arrived earlier had already made costumes out of the multi-colored materials, looking like something out of an Arabian Nights fantasy.

The woman responsible for putting the fabric there was an inner child therapist. Her plan was to lead us through some exercises to that effect later. But she had not counted on a group like ours. We were more likely in need of finding our outer adult. Without knowing why the material was there, people donned it automatically.

The way the performance night proceeded was simple. Whenever someone felt the impulse, they would just get up and start doing something.

Performance followed performance, everyone receiving a lot of enthusiastic support. Russian Passion was beginning to get impatient to perform. It was getting later and later and it was clear that the audience was fading. By the time we got to the stage, the novelty of what we were doing was the only thing that kept the others and ourselves awake. Once we got off the stage, there were only a couple more performances. Thankfully, they were brief and the evening ended.

* * *

I decided to skip gym class the next morning and instead of going to the morning meditation in the White Room, I went into the other meditation room where the afternoon sessions were held. It was pitch dark when the door shut automatically behind me so I began feeling around on the wall for a light switch. When I had finally groped my way to one and flicked it on, a large image of "Baba," the man who had organized this order, if you want to call it that, was illuminated. His kind face filled the entire wall/screen. It wasn't what I was hoping to see and certainly not what I wanted to meditate at. I couldn't help thinking how much his likeness resembled Frank Morgan's in ***The Wizard of Oz***. I had hoped to activate one of the pinpoints of light screens and have my own moment of meditation, but couldn't find the right switch. I tried to give Baba a chance to inspire me but we weren't on the same wavelength. After a couple of minutes I gave up. I kept expecting someone to jump out and say, "Pay no . . . attention to that . . . man on the screen . . ."

There was to be no cafe discussion on this day. Instead, we were loaded into two busses and transported to the Healesville Sanctuary, an open, hands-on zoo which featured the country's largest collection of indigenous Australian animals. Since we had formed our nucleus, Beta, the three Russians and I boarded the first bus. Before long our laughter attracted attention and the people immediately surrounding us were leaning into our conversation to catch what they could, add what they could and enjoy the laugh with us. I had never spent so much time laughing in my life. This had gone on for three days now with no end in sight. It was absolutely therapeutic.

One of the objects of our going to Healesville was to meet with and have a private discussion with an Aboriginal man who worked there acquainting people with Aboriginal ways. We saw his presentation before meeting with him.

After his show, our group was ushered into a small theatre where we waited for him. For his show, he had painted his body in the traditional way with white lines and spots so when he came into the theatre wearing his own clothing, the paint was still visible where he wasn't covered. It felt like being back stage after any other show. But he soon proved himself to be more than just any other performer. He was an absolutely beautiful human being, warm, genuine and committed to teaching others about the ways of his people.

He began by telling us about himself. First of all, his people had at one time populated the very land now occupied by the sanctuary. His talk was intensely personal, but not in the least self-conscious or bitter. Like everyone on the planet, he had his share of ups and downs but it was clear that he had a spiritual foundation which brought him through it all. His spiritual foundation was based on the old Aboriginal ways. They obviously meant everything to him.

We learned that his mother is the elder of their tribe and he was to be the next elder. There were only three members and yet they thought of themselves as a people. The rest had been decimated long ago. Their language has never been documented and never will be. I had asked about this and his answer was that some clerk had insulted his mother years ago in regard to her language. At that moment she decided it would never be written for others to know. When her line died, so would the language. He told us he would honor his mother's decree since she is the elder. The language will die with his daughter, who is also knowledgeable about her people's ways and embraces her Aboriginal heritage entirely.

It is not unusual for people to make the mistake of comparing Aboriginal Australians to African Americans, owing to the similarity of their skin color. However, the more meaningful comparison is to Native Americans. Aboriginal people have lived on the land known as Australia for upwards of 40,000 years. They, like their American counterparts, have a respect for the land itself which requires that they live in harmony with it, using it, living off it, but never presuming to own it. To Aboriginal people, land represents spirit, whereas with Europeans it represents wealth. Over those 40,000 years the original Australians developed medicines from the native plants and found food everywhere. After we had finished our time together in the theatre, he took us on a nature walk around the grounds, pointing out a number of plants and what they were used for. Many were edible, some were used for a variety of medicinal purposes including one which would terminate an unwanted pregnancy. Obviously things have not significantly changed in the past 40,000 years or so.

When Europeans came to Australia, eventually they wanted to make it into Europe. In addition to imposing their social customs, they introduced many plants and animals which have completely disrupted Australia's natural balance. There are camels in the large expanses of desert which make up Australia's middle. These were imported for obvious reasons and then left to run wild. There are wild pigs which descended from animals carried as food by Captain Cook. Other animals were brought for various reasons: donkeys as beasts of burden, foxes so the English gentry could hunt them in the traditional way, rabbits and deer for similar reasons, water buffalo to pull wagons. Imported frogs and carp clog many waterways. All these animals have altered the habitat. The amazing variety of animals which naturally populates this island continent is found nowhere else on the planet. One of the most interesting and, perhaps, telling things about Oz is that apart from the dingo, there are no other predatory mammals. This peaceful land existed, virtually as is, for thousands and thousands of years until the nineteenth century.

In their zeal to make Australia more "home like," the white people who came to this country, both voluntarily and as convicts, destroyed acres and acres of trees to clear land for sheep and crops, without any concern for the natural environment. And in their place they planted other vegetation from back home. One can understand that in their ignorance, these settlers would intend to conquer the land, as it were. In many cases the land has accepted and adjusted to these changes. However, more and more people nowadays are replanting their gardens and land with indigenous flora in an attempt to reestablish that natural environment and reclaim Australia's uniqueness.

Similarly, the early settlers destroyed most of the Aboriginal population which was located around the eastern and southern coasts. In Tasmania they were slaughtered to extinction. The settlers tried to turn the rest of the Aboriginal people into poor copies of themselves, eventually criticizing them for not being able to assimilate.

As he talked to us about the traditions and culture of his remote past, and the horrors his and other peoples had suffered, from time to time, he would brush back a tear. He confessed to crying in any number of circumstances. He was so open and comfortable about this side of himself that it was lovely to see. He told us that he had made friends with a Native American, either a Navajo or an Apache, I don't remember which. In any case, this man has moved to and is living in Australia with an Aussie wife. Predictably, the two men hit it off and exchanged information about their individual, tribal ways. The Native American had told him that in his culture, when a man cries, it means that he is closer, at that moment, to the Great Spirit than at any other time.

Before long, he was asking us questions. After all, he was in the midst of an international cultural exchange and was as eager to learn about some of our people as we were to learn about him. We stayed there for nearly two hours. In the most spontaneous moment of the afternoon, Sushi did an impromptu dance, without musical accompaniment, only the sounds of her bare feet on the stage and rhythmic sounds from her mouth.

Several rainbows marked our way on the ride back to the retreat center. Rainbows are a phenomenon of this country called Oz. Sometimes I think of Australia as "over the rainbow." The references to rainbows and Oz are constant. Traveling in the company of multiple rainbows with these people from all around the planet merely seemed appropriate.

* * *

That evening many of us congregated in the music area.

Anna, whose primary way of interacting with all of us was through her fingers on the piano keys, pounded out a tango so that Mimi, the Argentinean, could properly teach those who wished to learn. Beta and Naya, Dutch, an Aussie from Italy, Sydney, Falsetto, Sushi, Lydia and a few others gathered around and either danced or watched.

While this activity was in full swing, people were beginning to think of the end of the retreat. As it got later, people tended to drift off to their rooms. But a few of us weren't ready to let go yet. We found out that it was Dutch's birthday and eight of us decided to take a midnight stroll around the grounds in celebration. Dutch, Sydney, Beta, Naya, Betty, Bob (a musician whom I'd spoken to briefly), Sushi and I quietly made our way to the path which led away from the main building. It was a crystal clear night and thousands of stars were visible. Sushi was looking up at the sky in search of the three stars she had pointed out to her husband in India. She had told him that any time he saw them from that moment on they would remind him of her. Instinctively, I knew that the three stars in question were a part of the constellation Orion, the only one in this southern hemisphere sky which I recognized, even though it was upside down. I found Orion and asked if those were the stars she meant. They were. For a moment I was lost in my own thoughts. Orion had always meant something special to me too. I always looked for it wherever I was.

Sydney and Dutch found a wide, flat place on the path where she threw down a blanket she had brought along. We spread out, each of us claiming small portions of it. Bob and Betty were carrying on a private discussion on astronomy and quantum physics and novas and galaxies and I don't know what all which was so detailed and erudite that it belonged in academia. Dutch, Sydney, Beta, Naya, Sushi and I were more earthbound, on our backs, looking up at the endless sky. Before long we were spotting shooting stars and trying to point them out to one another before they burned out. It was a Golden Moment. We all felt connected to each other and the Universe.

* * *

Our last full day began a little later for me. I slept in, missing both exercise and the morning's meditation. I was not alone. As the days passed, more and more people were missing some of the early activities. Those who were dedicated to this discipline were, predictably, the more reliable ones.

After breakfast we were to have our final cafe meeting. There was a smaller table in the back of the room which caught my eye. Sally and Sydney were already seated there. As I hadn't spent any time with Sally since we first arrived, I seated myself at this table. By the time our session began, Bob, from the night before, Falsetto, a guy named Pete whom I'd spent very little time with, and Sushi had joined us.

This day's topic was "PURPOSEFUL DEDICATION: WHAT SPIRITUAL QUALITY WOULD I LIKE TO OFFER TO THE WORLD THROUGH MY ART? TO WHAT PURPOSE DO I DEDICATE MY LIFE?" Since it was already difficult for me to think of or refer to myself as an artist, classifying what I did as "art" was a bridge I couldn't cross. I began fumferring about it when Falsetto said he had an idea. It was as if he read my mind.

"I'm not very comfortable talking about myself in this way," he began. "What if we did something a little different?"

"Like what?"

"Why don't we take this time to tell each other what kind of impression they've made on us, not an evaluation, but a kind of insight into how we have projected ourselves?"

Everyone liked the idea. It was immediately clear that we had left strong impressions on each other. The group began talking about Sally and I realized the validity of peoples' observations. I knew her. When people began speaking of the qualities they saw in her, of her openness and kindness and intelligence and sparkling personality and other things which I knew to be strong and specific character traits, I saw that they also knew her. We spoke the Truth to one another and as a result, beautiful, spontaneous emotion punctuated with tears and laughter followed. We all got very close to the Great Spirit that morning. It was another Golden Moment. When, at the end of the session, each table summarized its discussion, the entire room was envious of what we had done. It had been so spontaneous and honest and lovely that everyone understood its magic.

The afternoon was ours to do with what we pleased. I had decided to take a walk to the Shell station for an ice cream and offered to buy one for whoever came along. Our little safari included Lydia, Beta, Naya, Sushi and myself. It was a leisurely stroll filled, of course, with laughter. At one point I stood back and just looked at these people: an Indian woman in a sari, an African woman in a colorful dashiki, a Russian girl with flashing, dark eyes, a German man with a shaved head and wire glasses and me, a Yank Down Under. It seemed especially significant that this gathering had taken place in Australia. If it had taken place somewhere in America, the overpowering nature of the culture may have been too influential, may have dominated too much. I could not nor would not ever deny my American heritage. The principles on which America was founded resonate with me every day. But because it is so dominant, one can lose perspective, particularly about the rest of humanity which doesn't share the same political and social origins. Being in another country provides that perspective and makes one conscious that the world doesn't stop at New York or California. And furthermore, the rest of the world is filled with people who want to live full, meaningful lives whatever that means to them, who feel pain when someone or something is lost, who feel joy at achieving something, pride when someone else does, all the human emotions that all human beings feel that have nothing to do with nationality, ethnicity, beliefs or customs. I loved the idea that I was sharing this experience with people from all around the globe and finding so much common ground with them.

Everyone had ice cream except Sushi who had never tasted any dairy products in her life. She had a fruit juice. Lydia, true to her new, uninhibited self, demanded that I buy her a stuffed bear which was wearing a Shell logo. I was unable to resist and asked the other two women if they'd like one too. Neither had Lydia's brass and, therefore, declined. On the way back to the retreat, it was more of the same: laughter, teasing and play.

After dinner, we were asked to go outdoors to The Circle where we'd done our morning exercises. It was to be another of those moments which I inwardly cringed at because the object was to just be spontaneous. We were to do whatever came into our heads, hearts, gut or whatever. Some drums and other percussion instruments were taken out on which to make the rhythm for this spontaneity. As apprehensive as I was, I still picked up a drum and joined in.

Before long, I was once again proven to be too cynical. The entertainment flowed. Virtually everyone participated. One of the highlights, one of those moments when you wish you had a video camera, came when Beta and Sara performed an improvisational, totally reckless dance. It was so wild and done with such abandon that it looked choreographed. It was a brilliant moment which lives only in the memories of those of us who saw it. They took up practically all the space available in this huge circle and threw themselves around like rag dolls. I knew it was especially meaningful for Beta because despite the crush that Naya had on him, he had privately focused, without success, on Sara the entire time. The entertainment went on until nearly eleven o'clock, much later than most people had stayed together before. It was clear that everyone was aware of the imminent end to our time together.

Back inside, us die hards sat around the dining room talking and laughing. There were a few people in the music area. Anna was playing for Sara while she sang, "Moon River." Others were thumping or tinkling the percussion instruments. The music became a background for the various conversations in the dining room until another magical moment happened. Naya had brought her violin to the music area and began to play. There was someone else at the piano by now and he was reading the accompaniment in a book of violin solos she had brought with her.

Some of us gravitated to her sound and were rewarded by a rendition of Shubert's "Ave Maria." It was so moving and mesmerizing that all talking stopped. To add to this Golden Moment, Beta began dancing. His normally angular style became fluid and gracefully serious and captured perfectly what the violin was singing. When it finally ended, everyone was silent for a moment longer, holding their private reactions inside. Each of us was elevated by this experience. It was simply stunning and gorgeous and came from another world.

On the morning of our last day, after breakfast, we gathered in the White Room. Without structure, we began expressing what this experience had meant to us. People were encouraged to speak their feelings. People all expressed themselves as best they could. No matter how articulate or shy anyone may have been, the spirit of what they communicated was the same, that this gathering had had a profound impact on them.

Beta was the one who named some of the times as Golden Moments. For him, Naya playing the "Ave Maria" had been one which took him to another plane of existence and compelled him to express himself through dance. Each of us had at least one such experience. There were many tears shed during out last formal moment together. The most poignant moment may have been when a young man who had hardly made a contribution for the entire five days suddenly began speaking.

"I lost both my parents when I was fourteen. They died in a car crash and I never got to say goodbye. I've always wondered if I'd feel anything from them again. Just now, as you were all talking about how much this has meant to you, I felt my parents. I felt their love . . . right here in this room with you. I want to thank you for that." Tears were streaming down his cheeks and those of many others, mine included.

Just before it ended, someone asked if there was something in the Green Book for us. I found something which certainly summarized the experience for me:

"If you don't take a chance, you don't have a chance."

* * *

Some time has passed since that final moment. My life has been enriched by an experience I could have easily missed. I often think about that. If I hadn't met these people, if I hadn't taken advantage of the opportunity which was presented, I may never have known the difference. Things would have undoubtedly cruised along as they had before. But how poor in comparison I would have been. I would not have developed a friendship with Maddy. I hardly spent a private moment with her at the retreat. Yet now, she is one of my closest and dearest friends. I would not be hearing from Berlin on a regular basis, keeping up with the Butoh and related activities going on there. I would not have been awakened with a birthday greeting from Mumbai. I would not have heard a brilliant, young violinist in her first Melbourne concert. I would not have attended a particular esoteric dance recital. Surely, I could have gotten by without them. But having had them, knowing them, having experienced these moments and these individuals has enriched my life.

One of the things that people said to me when we sat at that little table during the last cafe session was that they perceived me as a rich person, not rich in financial terms but rich in life experiences and relationships. How they could know this after such a brief encounter amazes me. Because it is the truth. I have always measured my wealth in those terms. It is clear to me that, in retrospect, I would be much the poorer, much the loser, much less complete without those moments of pure gold which I experienced by just saying yes.

THE ST. VALENTINE'S DAY NUGGET

I had met Nugget several weeks before. He was a man in his thirties, strong as a tree and gentle as a puppy, a New Age man spliced to a hard scrabble, fair dinkum Aussie bloke.

That first afternoon, when Nugget began telling me about his exploits in the gold fields west of Ballarat, he dropped two lumps of gold into my hands, lumps that he had brought out of the ground. They felt magical as they rested heavily in each of my palms. I had never seen, let alone felt, pure gold taken from the earth in exactly its shape. Pure, pristine, shiny, golden gold. Only an idiot would wonder what all the fuss was about.

I saw Nugget a time or two after that, once walking along Chapel Street in Melbourne and once at a party which was held at the house he shared with his two nieces, one of whom was in **The Great Gatsby** with me and the reason I'd met Nugget in the first place. On the Chapel Street occasion, we ended up going to a movie together and it was that night that a much longed for secret wish came true. Ever since Nugget had dropped those two lumps in my hand, I wanted to experience the quest for gold for myself.

There were friends visiting me from California who would be leaving just before Valentine's Day weekend. One of the places I'd taken them was Ballarat. I did it for two reasons. Firstly, I knew they would love seeing this unique place, its beautifully preserved Victorian buildings which were built after the Gold Rush days of the 1850's and the impressive restoration of Sovereign Hill where gold was actually processed, complete with its Chinatown, school, smelting facilities, candle and furniture and clothing makers, a complete community with dirt floor dwellings and the smell of gold all around it.

That was the second reason I took them to Ballarat. I wanted to immerse myself in a sense of gold, a consciousness of gold, receptiveness to gold. I wanted to look again at the replicas of some of the most massive nuggets of gold ever found on this planet. One, Welcome Stranger, had been discovered when the wheel of a passing wagon got stuck in the mud and hit an obstacle the size of a respectable boulder made of solid gold. There were others, some of equal size, some slightly smaller and some even larger. I wanted to be ready in every sense of the word when Nugget called.

My friends left Melbourne on Friday morning. Nugget called me the next day.

"How's it goin', mate? What do you reckon?"

"I'm ready," I said.

"I think we'd better give it go then. I'll just organize m' gear and swing by for ya."

"What do I need to bring?" I had no idea what kind of accommodations to expect.

"If you've got a doona, that'd be good. There's beds and sheets. No worries there. Just bring along a doona if you want."

I packed a pair of shorts and a couple of tee shirts, wore a pair of jeans and a new, organic cotton top that my friends had brought from L.A. (a garment which immediately became known to me as my gold mining shirt), my shaving kit, even though I had no intention of shaving, and a book just in case.

As we approached the village of Chaney (that's not the real name, but it's close enough), a village populated by about 350 people, Nugget began talking to me about gold.

"Now, y' see where those noses are. That's where the water flowed – around that way. These were massive rivers at one time. These were all riverbeds. And the gold, bein' heavy, would just move this much distance in a thousand years." He held his thumb and index finger within an inch of one another. "Maybe it'd get stuck behind somethin' and rest there and wait for some lucky bloke to come along and find it. You can see over there where they've done some diggin'. Those big holes held gold, more than likely. Looks like gold was all down through there."

As we got closer to Chaney, Nugget pointed out places where he'd found gold himself. "There's lots of gold out here for the bloke who wouldn't mind puttin' in a little work. I'd like to come out to some of these places with a backhoe or some big diggin' equipment. Probably another Welcome Stranger down there, I reckon."

We arrived at Chaney and pulled into Nugget's driveway. He owned a very new looking brick house, in excellent condition even though it was actually quite old, more than a hundred years. There were three bedrooms, a lounge room, kitchen, indoor toilet and shower. Nugget had a deep well of rainwater that was the envy of his neighbors, and had the availability of "city" water as well. Behind the house were several connected, wooden structures which started out as buildings at the end near the house but which deteriorated into a shaky-roofed lean-to as it progressed to the other end. There were lots of cuttings planted in large pots scattered around and about, some doing better than others. One pink flower bloomed all by itself in the corner of what appeared to be a casually attended garden.

"Gotta spend at least a week or so out here," Nugget said. "Can't make it very homely when y' only get here a few days outa the month. But I got me some ideas and I'll fix 'er up one o' these days. I'd like to make a bed and breakfast place out of it and take city people and tourists out prospecting."

The lounge room was decorated with images of rock 'n' roll past. A large photo of Elvis would have dominated except for a five-foot version of "licks," the red and silver tongue which identified the Rolling Stones. It occupied a large portion of wall adjacent to the fireplace. Other photos and posters of similar icons dotted the walls, the Beatles and Marilyn Monroe prominent among them. Nugget's large CD collection was proof that he liked his music but it wasn't limited to the past. He had recently discovered "techno" and was equally enthusiastic about it as he had at one time been about B.B. King.

There was no woman's touch anywhere to be found. Sneakers and boots lay where they had been shed. Used cups and glasses sat in the sink where they had been left after the last visit. Others were stacked at the side, having been washed at some time in the past, awaiting their tea bag or beer, as the case may be, some time in the future. We were roughing it, pure and simple.

Nugget must have called ahead a day or so before, informing some of his neighbors that he'd be coming in for a couple of days. Not long after we arrived and got settled, he told me that a man named Robert would be coming by. While Nugget was attending to something in the front part of the house, a car pulled into his driveway.

"You must be Robert," I said.

"Must I?" the educated voice replied.

"Are you Robert?" I asked.

"No, I'm Chips," he answered.

"Pleased to meet you, Chips. I'm Chris."

About that time, Nugget returned to the back of the house. "G'dye, mate. Meet my friend, Chris."

"We've met. Yank?

"Yep," I answered.

"Thought so," was Chips' non-committal reply.

"How 'bout a cuppa, mate?"

"I don't mind," Chips replied.

"How 'bout a cuppa, Chris?"

"Sounds good," I said.

Nugget went into the kitchen and put the electric kettle on, the modern version of a bush tradition. In the real bush, beyond the black stump, tea is brewed in a proper billycan, blackened by a thousand boilings on top of an open fire. When the water starts to bubble, you toss in a handful of tea and a handful of sugar and let them cook together. Bush tea is always drunk black, with sugar if there is any, but rarely with milk. Nugget soon brought out the contemporary version, three cups with tea bags dangling along with a canister of sugar.

Chips quickly proved himself to be a man without sharp edges. He was very well spoken and spent much of his considerable free time reading. He had grown up in Sydney and lived the city life most of his 60-some years. But what he called the rat race was too much for him. What other pressures may have also contributed to his isolation could only be guessed at. But he appeared to live happily on a pension in a trailer where he could go out and prospect now and again and read the rest of the time.

"I'm thinking about getting back into the rat race," he said, after we'd blown the hot off the top of our tea and taken a sip.

"How so?" I asked.

"I reckon I'll be moving in to Ballarat. Maybe I'll find something to do there. And find a woman."

"What kind of work would you do?"

"Oh, I don't know. I'll find something. I'm on a pension so I'd only want to do something a couple of days a week. But there's no women to be had here. That's my main reason for going."

"If you could do anything you wanted," I asked, "if someone touched you with a magic wand and said you can do whatever you want, what would it be?"

He thought for a while, took another sip of tea, thought some more, gazed out into the openness and answered methodically. "I reckon I'd like to work somehow for reconciliation with the Aboriginals."

This was one of the things I loved about Australia. There is beneath it all a fundamental spirit of generosity and good will which surfaces in the most unexpected and gratifying places. Here was this man who lived in the bush on practically nothing for a number of years and if he could do anything in the world, would try to find a way to heal the wound which exists as the only blemish in the country's remarkably peaceful history. I have come across this kind and quality of thinking many times in my conversations and travels around Oz. And it has no economic or class origin. It's a matter of doing the right thing, a philosophy which permeates every level of society.

"Yeah, you city boys don't know what it's like out here with no women," Chips lamented once more. Then, as if to punctuate his remark, he let go the most earth rattling, Vesuvian belch, one that started with a rumble low in the belly and erupted to the surface and rolled along and lingered like thunder on a summer night.

"Whoops," he said. "Shame on you, Jingles. How rude of you." He shook his finger at his little dog. Jingles looked up for a moment on hearing his name and then returned to what he had been doing before the volcano erupted.

We finished our tea in a leisurely fashion. Nugget and Chips broke the silence every so often with an observation about someone in Chaney or a chore that needed doing around Nugget's place or where they thought gold could be found or any number of different, unconnected subjects that drifted to the surface in its laconic way. It reminded me of the joke about the three hermits, living in a cave together. A horse passed by the front of the cave. Hermit #1, several days later says, "Did you see that black horse?" A year passes. Hermit #2 says, "It was a brown horse." Another eight months pass. Hermit #3 says, "If you don't stop this constant bickering, I'm leaving." Thus it was with Nugget and Chips. There was no hurry about anything. Aside from these infrequent attempts at conversation, the only thing that disturbed our tranquillity were three more well developed emissions from Chips.

After a little while Chips decided that it was time for a beer and wandered to a bottle shop to bring back a couple of liters. While he was gone, Nugget showed me around the place. We walked to the front yard.

"Y'see this here?" There was some fairly fresh horse manure just behind the low fence which separated his yard from the footpath. "Somebody would've thrown that over here. One o' me neighbors, most likely. They do that sort of thing. Probably thought me grass could use a bit of fertilizing. People tend to come by and look after the place a bit. Chips waters me plants now and again."

As we strolled around to the back of the house, he showed me a room that he wanted to make into a studio.

"What kind of studio?" I asked.

"Aw, I don't know. Maybe put in a kiln."

"You make pottery?"

"I'm thinkin' about it. It might be a nice thing to do. Get a bit creative."

Chips was soon back with the beers and we sat around a wooden table which was outside the back door just off the verandah. We sat there drinking our beers in silence, looking up through the trees at a brilliant blue sky and listening to the magpies argue about something or other as they chased back and forth in the treetops.

It was getting along about dusk when Nugget broke the silence. "I reckon we ought to have a feed. What do you reckon, Chris?"

"Fine by me. I haven't eaten today except for some fruit this morning."

"How 'bout you, Chips? Want to join us for a chop?"

"Where are you going?" Chips asked.

I wouldn't have thought there was any choice in Chaney. I had taken a little stroll to find a pay phone during the previous silent period and had covered the entire town in about ten minutes. I saw one other place that looked like it could be a restaurant and had a restaurant's name, something like The Bull and Horn. It was in an old building and it was hard to work out if it was still a functioning establishment or a remnant of better days.

"I reckon we'll go to the pub," Nugget replied.

"What about that place, The Bull and Something?" I asked. "I noticed it on my walk just now."

Chips was quick to respond. "Too bloody pricey."

Out of curiosity I would like to have learned what Chips considered expensive. With the exception of petrol, everything seemed to be much less expensive in country towns. But his objection was so swift and uncompromising that I said nothing.

"I reckon we'll go to the pub then," Nugget repeated. "No rush, mate. Let's finish our beers."

The interior of the pub was like the interior of every other pub I've seen in Australia. That is to say that it was non-descript. It had the compulsory bar room complete with a television up in one corner and a few tables and chairs, stools along the bar. A common sort of foyer connected the bar with the dining room, the obligatory billiard room and the toilets. The dining room was relatively large, suggesting that most of the residents of Chaney must have eaten there on a regular basis at one time during its history.

Chaney had had its own boom back when. It was nothing like Ballarat's, not nearly so large. But it had been sufficient for a little community to develop around it and survive, in an area known as the Golden Triangle. Other towns in the vicinity had had a moment of glory and virtually turned to dust, eroded and blown away by time. But not Chaney. Besides the pub, there was a town hall, post office, a couple of empty church structures, a jail and another old building which was now the Chaney Museum. All these buildings were made either of Victoria's famous blue stone or of brick and had been around for well over one-hundred--twenty-five years. Nugget told me that he was a member of the Historical Society which wanted to preserve as much of Chaney's past as possible and maybe even turn it into a tourist stop. There were already signs posted strategically around town, pointing out places of interest.

No sooner had we walked into the pub than the "Yank" jokes began. The first person I met was a man named Jim. It was very early evening so Jim's condition was either a result of his having been there since morning or he was in a constant state of inebriation. Either would have been possible.

"How you goin', Jim? This is a mate of mine, Chris."

"How you doing?" I reached for Jim's hand. Instead, he put his arm around my shoulder and hugged me. He held on to me for a very long moment and when I moved to release myself, he moved with me, holding on for dear life.

"You're not a fuckin' Yank, are ya?" Jim asked. "That's not a fuckin' Yank accent you've got, is it, mate?"

"Yes, but I'm planning to give it up for Lent," I answered.

Jim must have thought that was a good answer because he howled with laughter. "D'ya hear that? He says he's giving up 'is accent f' Lent." And with that he hugged me again. Jim was what we would have called a harmless drunk back in Ohio, where I grew up in the States. All love and hugs and touching when allowed, but otherwise not threatening.

"Reckon we'd better have a beer," Nugget suggested.

We moved up to the service window of the bar and ordered our beers. The barman looked at me as if I'd dropped in from Pluto. He had one eye sort of squinched shut while the other was wide open. His hair was very close cropped and several tattoos were visible on his skeletally thin arms. "You like Australian beer, mate?"

"I used to drink Fosters in New York, when I lived there."

"Aw, mate, we don't drink that horse piss here. We send it all overseas to the Yanks."

"Well, then I'll have what you drink here," I said. The barman's squinched up eye opened a little while the other one widened and a careful, barely perceptible smile broke out along his mouth. Nugget gave me a surreptitious wink of approval and we took our beers into the dining room.

An attractive young woman came out of the kitchen. Jim introduced her to all of us. She had obviously begun working at the pub since Nugget's last visit to Chaney. It wasn't possible for anyone to go unnoticed in this community, especially a woman. Chips eyed her with great interest even though she was at least forty years his junior. I asked her what I should order. I figured that I'd get the freshest or best on offer that way. She suggested the T-bone steak. In the midst of all these Aussie blokes, I didn't want to confess out loud that I tended to stay away from red meats. It was enough of a blemish just being a Yank. Being a vegetarian in the bargain would have lost me what little credibility I might have gained.

"Well, I – uh – maybe – uh – " I fumferred.

She caught my drift. "What about the seafood platter. People tend to like that," she offered.

"Sounds perfect." I said.

Not long after, a group of six people came into the dining room. By the looks of things they were a family. I didn't pay much attention to them at first. Jim went immediately among them and greeted them with the same affection that he'd shown me. Nugget and Chips nodded hello and I sort of glanced back at them over my shoulder.

One of them was very loud, a teenager. At first I thought he was just undisciplined and rude, but the quality of his voice had something else in it. When I got up to get another round of beers, I had a better look at the young man in question. He was big but not fat. He seemed very high strung and it took virtually all their effort for the adults to keep him contained. Jim was teasing and playing with him in a good-natured way. Before anyone knew what happened, the boy spun Jim to the floor and landed on top of him with his full weight. The father lightly chided the boy and coaxed him to his feet. Jim had a grin on his face when he got up off the floor. It hadn't affected him in the least.

As I was waiting for the barman to pour my beers, a bearded face pushed up next to mine. It belonged to a man who looked to be in his thirties. His beard was one of those Wolfman types where hair occupies every available centimeter of space, so that only a little cheek, forehead, lips and ears showed. He had a most angelic expression in his eyes.

"Is that a Yank accent?" he asked.

"Yep," I answered. "Sure is."

"What's a bloody Yank doin' here in Chaney?"

"Just passing through, spending some time with a friend from Melbourne."

"You know what we think of Yanks here, don't you?" His expression was still angelic but his tone was changing.

It brought to mind an observation about American GI's made by Australian men during World War II. They used to complain that American servicemen were over paid, over sexed and over here.

"I wouldn't know," I said, "but only my accent is Yank. I'm an Aussie now." Before any more dialogue, my beers arrived. I picked them up and started away.

"Hey, wait a minute, you fuckin' Yank. I'm not finished with you yet."

"I've got some food in there and my mates are waiting for their beers. I'm not going anywhere. I'll talk to you later," I said and returned to the dining room.

We finished our meal and walked toward the poolroom. It was open to the night air and about four thousand varieties of flying bugs fluttered in to get close to the florescent light which illuminated the pool table, dropping dead or nearly so in such numbers that their carcasses affected the roll of the balls. There was a couple playing what was obviously a game of Eight Ball except the balls had no numbers on them. Seven were yellow, seven were pinkish and one was an ominous black. I sipped my beer and watched them play.

Both were rather large people and pretty good pool players. It's one of the areas in Australia where the playing field between men and women is level. Because pubs are a way of life in Oz, you'll find as many enthusiastic, good pool players in one sex as in the other. This couple was typical. But as I watched them between shots I realized that they spoke in sign language, making an occasional grunt for emphasis. They were having a terrific time teasing one another, sipping their beers and shooting pool. It was the kind of thing that might call attention to itself somewhere else, but here in this little town of Chaney, it was no big deal, no different than taking a family member who was mentally handicapped out for an evening.

Nugget asked me if I wanted to shoot a game of pool. I warned him that my youth was not misspent and I wasn't much of a pool player, but that I was willing to give it a go. He put a dollar coin on the edge of the table and we waited our turn.

When the man knocked in the black ball by accident, their game was finished and we stepped up.

"Fuckin' Yanks don't know how to shoot pool. I'll show you how to shoot bloody pool!" It was the voice of the angelic eyed, bearded one. He had found me. Still smiling he picked a cue for himself. "Me and this bloke will take yuz on. And we're gonna kick yer arse."

"You wouldn't be the first," I said and reached for the rack.

"Yeah, and you won't be the first Yank that got his arse kicked by me either," he taunted.

"I believe you," I said as neutrally as possible. Whereas Jim was what we called a harmless drunk back in Ohio, this guy was a nasty drunk, belligerent and aggressive, all the while wearing his angelic expression. I decided to defer when possible.

As the game progressed, Angel Eyes grew more confident. "Fuckin' Yanks can't shoot pool. Who fuckin' told you you could shoot pool, Yank?" He was surprisingly good. Or perhaps not so surprising since he must have spent most of his waking hours in some kind of drinking establishment, most of which have pool tables. Nugget kept us in the game. I had one run of three balls which I knew to be an accident but looked good nonetheless. When it came down to making the black ball, you could have easily gotten the impression that no one wanted to win. Player after player missed. When it came Angel Eyes turn again, he looked up at the jukebox which was playing "Don't Worry, Be Happy" by Bobbie McFarrin.

"I hate that fuckin' song. Turn that fuckin' thing off," he yelled at no one in particular. When no one responded to his demand, Angel Eyes walked over to the jukebox and grabbed it with both arms, flinging it back against the wall with all his might and causing the song to cease. "That's better. Now, put some money in there," he demanded of the male member of the mute couple. The man smiled at him and indicated that he didn't have any change.

Angel Eyes looked at him for a moment before deciding that he wouldn't pursue it further. Then he announced, "I'm not takin' this bloody shot until someone plays some bloody music. I can't play without music." And with that he tucked the cue under his arm and waited with a Mussolini kind of arrogance. No one did anything. No one said anything. Time froze while Angel Eyes decided how far he was going to go with this. I made it a point not to make any eye contact with him. If I had, I felt sure I'd hear one of those *What are you lookin' at?* kind of remarks which left no room for a right answer.

Angel Eyes' partner put a coin in the juke box and played a funky, r & b tune which seemed to qualify as music to shoot pool by. The cue ball made contact with the black ball and the game was over.

"You owe us a beer," Angel Eyes announced.

Nugget said, "We didn't say we were playin' for a beer, mate."

"Hey, Yank, you owe me a fuckin' beer. I beat yer arse. Now pay up."

"Beating my ass was no accomplishment. Anybody can do that," I said.

"Yeah, and I beat yer arse, didn't I? Now, where's me bloody beer?"

At this point, I felt that enough was enough. As a matter of principle I wasn't going to buy this guy a beer. We hadn't made a bet before starting the game and his bullying tactics were starting to get on my nerves. I remained under control but had made up my mind about his beer. If he wanted one, he could buy it himself.

Nugget, on the other hand, took a more diplomatic approach. He had slipped away to the bar and returned with two beers, one for Angel Eyes and one for his partner, who was obviously embarrassed.

"That's more like it," Angel Eyes said. "Now rack 'em up and we'll take yuz on again."

I looked at Nugget. His expression said, "Why not?" So I racked up the balls and then broke.

Again, the game was close and down to the black ball for both sides. Angel Eyes never stopped his rantings and insults and it was obvious that he was sticking it to anyone he could, but especially to me. You fuckin' Yanks aren't this and you fuckin' Yanks are that and on and on. As he was carrying on, I remembered a time in my dad's restaurant when this drunk kept repeating how much he didn't like Pop. "You've got a nice boy here, Mr. Wallace, but I don't like you." Over and over and over until Pop had reached the limit of his short span of tolerance and cold cocked the guy. I wasn't my father so I had no inclination to throw any punches. Instead, I just smiled and agreed with Angel Eyes as best I could.

Nugget went to the toilet leaving me alone with Angel Eyes. He had just taken a shot at the black ball and not only missed it, but scratched. That meant I had two shots coming according to Aussie rules. I missed with my first but left the cue ball in perfect position to sink the black ball. It looked intentional. It wasn't. A blind man could have made the next shot. Angel Eyes was quiet for once. I felt the weight of the world on my shoulders. The jukebox was silent. I aimed, slid the pool cue back and forth through my thumb and index finger and punched the cue ball. It cracked against the black ball and sent it gracefully into the corner pocket. I looked up at Angel Eyes and smiled. I wanted to ask him if he was buying this round, but bit my tongue. He threw his stick on the table and muttered something. I found Nugget and Chips and we left.

Out in the street, Chips said, "He's a nasty piece of work, that one."

"Thought he was kicked outa the pub," Nugget said.

"That was by the old owners," Chips answered. "These new ones are giving him the benefit of the doubt. They'll throw him out soon."

"Why? What's the deal with Angel Eyes?" I asked.

"He tends to get into fights pretty easily," Chips said, "pushes people 'til they've got no choice. He's pretty mean when he's drunk."

"Yeah, he was on his good behavior tonight, mate," Nugget said to me. "Otherwise, you'd have had yer hands full, I reckon, bein' as how you were a new bloke and a Yank in the bargain."

"Oh, great," I said. "That's all I need."

"You handled yerself, mate." Nugget said. "You didn't give him the chance to push you into a corner. Besides, I was lookin' out for ya. No worries."

"What about that kid that was rough housing with Jim?" I asked.

"Aw, he's not quite right in the head. But he's a nice kid," Nugget said.

"That was dangerous when he threw Jim to the floor," Chips added. "That made me wince a bit."

"Right," Nugget said. Then he turned to me. "Jim was a quadriplegic."

"What?" I was incredulous. "What do you mean?"

"Fair dinkum. He had an accident to his spinal cord and was paralyzed from the neck down. Somehow or other it healed. He's a medical marvel, a miracle, really." Chips said. The picture of the kid slamming Jim to the floor replayed in my mind.

"Unbelievable," I said. I had enough knowledge about quadriplegia to know that it was indeed a miracle. One of the first things I did when I first moved to Australia was produce a benefit for Quadriplegic Hand Foundation at the Victorian Arts Centre.

* * *

The next morning, Sunday, Valentine's Day, I heard some stirring in another room. I looked at my watch and saw that it was 8 a.m. I pulled on a pair of shorts and a tee shirt and walked out of my bedroom. Chips had the kettle going.

"Thought I'd have to wake you buggers up," Chips said cheerily.

"Good mornin', mate," Nugget said as he stumbled into the kitchen. He looked like a man who is slow to wake up and even less eager to do so.

"Cuppa?"

"Yeah, mate." Nugget answered. "There's coffee there somewhere too if you like."

Within twenty minutes, we had drunk our tea and were out the door. Chips had advised me to change into long pants because of some briars that might be found where we were going. I also slipped on my gold mining shirt. Just before we got in the car, I took my lucky coin out.

"Heads, we find gold," I announced and tossed it into the air. I caught it and slapped it onto the top of my left hand.

"What's it say?" Nugget asked.

I looked. "We're going to find gold," I assured them. And off we went.

We left the main road for another which was paved but only one lane wide and then found our way into the bush on a dirt track. We had to pass through a gate on the way into this deeper bush. "That'd be yer job, mate," Nugget said as he eased the car to a stop. "And always leave it as you found it. That's a rule in the bush."

I thought to myself, *What a reasonable credo. Leave it as you found it.* What would the condition of the planet be if we had practiced such a simple notion through the ages? The rivers would still run clean. Mining areas wouldn't look like moon craters. Forests would still produce oxygen. How novel.

I opened the gate and then closed it, struggling to replace the wire which held it in exactly the way I found it. I had not paid enough attention to how it came undone. I did the best I could then got back in the car. "The next guy is not going to know that I didn't do it right," I said. "But it is secure and as long as he leaves it as he found it, it'll be all right." It then occurred to me that I could sometimes be a bit too literal.

Before long we were off that more or less well-traveled dirt track and on to another which was barely discernible. It reminded me of a time in Kenya when we were trying to find our way back from a safari encampment. During the light hours, the track was nearly invisible. At dusk, when we were traveling, the game warden I was with had to stand on the seat and look out through the top of the Land Rover for tire tracks. The Australian bush often reminded me of East Africa. Trying to follow this track was just another example.

We twisted our way deeper into the bush to a location which Chips had inspected some time earlier and thought might prove interesting. Nugget had talked about another area but was game to try this one. I had no opinion.

We pulled the car to a stop in a clearing and began to unload. Chips' little dog, Jingles, jumped to the ground and began sniffing as if he was looking for gold too. Both Chips and Nugget pulled their metal detectors from the boot of their cars and Nugget pointed down at the pickax. "That's yers, mate. You'll be my digger."

Another person may have thought that was demeaning, but the term "digger" is so Australian that those graced with it are legendary. It has the charm of being called "cowboy" by a Montana cattleman. It's a term of endearment, of history, of respect. I swelled up with pride as I picked up my digging tool. If it had been a movie, you'd have heard "Waltzing Matilda" playing softly in the background. I slung the pickax over my shoulder, puffed out my chest and off we went, Chips to one area with Jingles and Nugget to another with his Digger.

After we'd walked for a little while, Nugget waving his metal detector along the ground and me following with the pick on my shoulder, Nugget stopped. He kicked a little dirt from the ground and said, "Have a little dig here, mate." All I heard was "dig" and I went at it with a vengeance. I was on my way to China when Nugget stopped me. "Mate, all you have to do is take some of this top dirt away. Let the tool do the work. Let the weight of it do yer diggin'. Like this." His demonstration was so skilled and practiced that I was embarrassed. Imagine not being able to use a pickax properly. I took his suggestions on board and tried to emulate his example from then on.

Nugget walked around slowly, brushing the ground gently with the surface of his metal detector. The headset was fitted loosely around his head so that when he came across any kind of metal, I could also hear its reaction.

"Y'see these trees here, these blackened ones?" Nugget asked. "Those are iron bark trees." Somehow I thought that the trees got their name because of their black color and said something to that effect. "Naw, mate, those trees are black because they've been burnt. This bush catches fire now and then, like any forest. The thing about these iron bark trees is they run north and south. You can see 'em all along this line." I tried my best to see a straight line of trees. Again, I was reminded of Africa. The first morning I was in the bush there, everyone in the Land Rover, including an eight-year-old boy, was pointing out game just off the side of the track. I couldn't see anything and suspected they might be pulling my leg, like going on a snipe hunt. After an adjustment period, my eyes began to see the well-camouflaged animals. I looked for a line of iron bark trees running north and south with no success, but nodded anyway. "There'll be gold around here," Nugget said.

He went back to his listening. As he scanned the ground, I looked around at the trees. It was a crystal clear day and the blue sky could be seen up through the leaves. I glanced down at one point and saw my shadow, one knee bent slightly, one hand on a hip, the other holding the handle of the pickax which was resting on my shoulder. It was the classic silhouette of a Digger, poised and ready to unearth a treasure. I took a mental picture of it and looked for it repeatedly throughout the rest of the morning.

"Dig a bit out here, mate," Nugget said. "Make it about this size." He indicated about a square foot area. I went to where he was and scraped off the dirt about four or five inches deep. In the meantime, Nugget was listening in another area.

"Ready," I said.

Nugget came back to my diggings. As he approached the area and passed his detector over it, I heard this loud "**WOW**!" sound. It must have deafened Nugget.

"Mate," he said gently, "you have to keep that pick up off the ground when I'm listening." The metal of the pickax had set off the detector.

Again, I felt embarrassed at my stupidity. "Sorry."

"No worries, mate. It's yer first time."

He scanned the area where I'd dug. "Naw, it's nothin'. Just fill in yer hole." As he said this he kicked some of the dirt back into the hole I'd dug. I then filled in the rest and tamped it down under my boots. "Leave it the way you found it" rang in my ears.

The same procedure continued while Nugget worked the area. He'd mark an "x" on the ground. I'd dig away some dirt. He'd shake his head and I'd fill in the hole. One time we found an old nail. Another time a little piece of non-descript metal. Another time an old screwdriver. I did my job a little better as time wore on and soon was into the rhythm of the activity. It wasn't hard work. The digging didn't require a great deal of effort or energy since it was only superficial in most instances. Either Nugget would find the metal object which attracted his attention, like the nail or screwdriver, or he'd decide it was a false alarm and move on. I spent a lot of time admiring my surroundings, not to mention the Digger's shadow.

We were well into our routine. Nugget listened and marked a place. I scraped off a layer of dirt. He came back, listened again, shook his head and kicked a little dirt into the hole. I'd fill it in and we'd go on to the next. Then, suddenly Nugget's interest intensified.

"Give this a little scrape, mate," he said.

I took off about five inches of dirt where he indicated. He listened again in the spot where I dug. There was another "wow" that I could hear. "Take a little more away," he said. I did, pulling a mound of dirt toward me. He listened again and the sound was fainter until he moved the device toward the mound of loose dirt. "WOW!" it said. "It'll be there in that dirt," Nugget said with confidence.

He told me to take a handful of dirt, shift half of it into my other hand and wave it under the metal detector. I took a handful of dirt in my right hand, poured half of it into my left hand and held it under the metal detector. "WOW!"

"That's yer watch, mate. Take the dirt in your other hand and wave it under the detector." I wondered how stupid one man could be and sheepishly transferred the dirt to my other hand. There was nothing in it. "Take a bit more and do it again." I did and we heard the "Wow." "Take some of that and keep doing it until you find what yer lookin' for," he said.

I was as excited as a kid at Christmas. I finally narrowed the metal down to a small handful of dirt, picking out little chunks and pulverizing them between my thumb and index finger. Finally something had substance to it. I waved it under the metal detector. "WOW!"

"What've you got, mate?" Nugget asked.

It was a piece of lead shot, a beebee. "Nothing," I answered.

"Let's take a little break and see how Chips is makin' out," Nugget suggested.

We saw Jingles first. Chips was kicking dirt into a hole. "Some bastard's been here," he said. "There are unfilled holes all over the place here. Bloody bastards."

"Any luck?" Nugget asked.

"Only these holes," Chips replied. "How about you?"

"Naw, not yet. But Chris' coin said we'd find gold and I reckon we will. Let's give it another hour or so and then head in. The sun's starting to warm up a bit."

"Yep," Chips answered.

I followed Nugget to another area, near where we were before. We re-established our routine. He listened, marked the ground with an "x." I dug and filled in hole after hole. We had been at it for nearly the hour which we had designated as our cut off. I was getting hot and sticky and by then had even lost interest in the Digger's silhouette.

"Give this a go here, mate." Nugget had heard something. I went to where he was and scraped off a layer of dirt. When I finished, I pointedly brought the pick up to my shoulder while Nugget listened. Through his headset I could hear the "wow" sound as he passed over the area I'd just dug out. "Take a little more out here, mate." I scraped away some more. Nugget wasn't moving away to look for another place while I dug. He stayed there, looking down. "That's good," he said. Again I made sure to replace the pick on my shoulder. The "Wow" was louder as he passed the detector over my newest diggings. "Take a bit more off just here." I did as I was told. The suspense was palpable. We were both aware of it, both feeling it. "WOW!" the detector said. "Start pulling some of this dirt off with yer hands, mate. Easy now." I stuck my hands in the earth and scooped away a handful at a time, careful to hold it in my non-watch hand as I passed it under the metal detector. As I was about to reach for another handful of dirt, Nugget said, "Look there," pointing down near where my hand had just been.

And there, with the barest, tiniest, tip of shine showing, was a golden speck. I reached down and picked it up. It was covered with dirt so I did the only natural thing there was to do. I spit into my left palm and put the piece of gold in it to wash off the dirt.

"That'd be yers, mate. You keep that."

"Really?" I asked.

"Fair dinkum," Nugget replied.

It was a flat piece of pure gold, roughly two centimeters long and if you used your imagination, could say that it was in the shape of the state of California. Nugget reckoned that it weighed about 1 ½ grams. To me, it was Welcome Stranger. In that moment, I had made a real connection with the planet Earth which went back 160 million years, when this gold formed. This very piece of gold had been in the earth roughly in this place for that length of time until I picked it up. Its size and weight were irrelevant. It was gold and I had found it. Well, actually Nugget had found it, but I was the Digger. If I'd had my wits about me, I'd have shouted, "Eureka!" but I didn't. I just looked at it and handled it and felt its weight and looked at it some more.

"Let's have a look," Nugget said, bringing me out of my ecstasy. I handed it to him and he assessed its quality. "That's a nice little piece of gold, mate." He handed it back to me.

As I fondled it, I said, "Well, it may not be the size of Welcome Stranger but I've got a name for it just the same. I'm calling it The St. Valentine's Day Nugget."

"That's a good one," he agreed. Then he added, as an afterthought, "I like that coin of yers, mate. Don't lose it.

NEW YEAR'S EVE WITH NEFERTITI

Two years after the *Just Say Yes* New Year's Eve, I found myself back on the Gold Coast visiting my DJ friend. This was going to be the biggest New Year's Eve of my life experience. Well, maybe not the biggest but as far as mileposts were concerned, it would be the most numerically significant. It was to be the actual beginning of the Third Millennium, not the bullshit one that everyone celebrated the year before like a bunch of lemmings. It seemed that no matter how convincing or obvious the evidence, people insisted on calling the last year of the Second Millennium the first year of the Third. I recall reading somewhere that Mark Twain, who was still alive and listened to in those days, kept insisting at the end of the previous century that they missed that one by a year too. Obviously they weren't listening all that well. And still don't. It must be that people get stuck on the idea that turning over all those nines into zeros means the beginning of something rather than the end. I mean, you don't start counting at zero and go to nine, you start at one and go to ten. Duh! But I digress.

For some reason, I had always looked forward to this particular New Year's Eve, even from the time I was a little kid. It got fixed in my imagination as a moment of great significance in my life. I don't know what I expected to happen but the moment was pregnant with significance and possibilities and mystical importance for me, as if it would usher in something profound. And even though I made no particular plans to commemorate this numerical beginning, I couldn't help wondering what might unfold.

The Club where my DJ friend performed his musical magic was pretty much *the* spot on the Gold Coast. Over the two-year period of his residence he had introduced a relatively unsophisticated crowd to very sophisticated dance music, mixing in salsa and African tribal tracks with French, British and American brands of various house and garage styles, going from a Middle Eastern sounding wail to a classic 70's disco track, cutting them together like butter. He was more a musicologist and teacher than a conventional disk jockey. He could talk with easy authority about Shoenberg and Stravinsky in one breath and Dimitri of Paris and Kenny "Dope" Gonzales in the next. Every evening was a new show, produced spontaneously with peaks and valleys that took his audience on a six-hour ride they'd never forget, even if they didn't understand anything about it except the beat.

We prepared to go to The Club in the usual manner, no fanfare because of the date, no special vibes. Just another night. Except I had this lingering sense of excitement brewing internally.

New Year's Eves in general have always special for me. It had nothing to do with romance or anticipation or impending good. It had more to do with how I had celebrated the first ones of my recollection. Growing up in Ohio left me few opportunities to be together with my family. My dad owned a restaurant that was open 363 days a year and the entire family worked there. The exceptions were Christmas day and the first of January. Those were the two days when we were all together around the dining room table, when my mother got out the good china and silver and crystal, when other family friends and our few relatives would join us, when there would be some homemade wine in the decanter and a shot of cognac before the meal to stimulate the appetite. The meals were always sumptuous, cooked to perfection by my pop. Like a busman going for a drive on a holiday, Pop would cook at home for his family. The smells were intoxicating. The mood was festive. Twice a year.

But the special thing about New Year's Eve was that when everyone came home after closing the restaurant, we would gather around the table in the family room and stay up gambling until the wee hours. Even when I was very young, they'd wake me when they came home so I could be a part of this memorable family time. And I was allowed to gamble along with everyone else.

Mostly we played Black Jack. Our house rules provided that whoever got a Black Jack also won the deal, giving anyone a chance to be the "house" at one time or another. We paid for five cards under 21, double for Black Jack and you could hit or not hit as you wished, dealer or not. Bets were nickels and dimes, nothing bigger. So no one won too much or lost too much. Five bucks would have constituted a big win or a gigantic loss.

It was always so much fun to sit around the table, everyone joking and teasing, without the pressure of having to get an order out or clear the dishes from the booth in the corner or rush to the cash register. We were a family at leisure on these one night and two days each year.

And after we'd played cards for a while, it was time for the Greek tradition of cutting the *Vasilopita*, a round loaf of special sweet bread which was made at New Year's and Easter. After it was baked, a coin (in our case a dime) was inserted in the bottom. In our family the oldest male always did the cutting, one triangular piece for each family member plus one for the business and one for our home. Pop would quickly count how many pieces were to be cut and with Pythagorean precision cut exactly that many pieces, each within a fraction of the size of all the others. It didn't matter if he cut ten pieces or seventeen, they were all absolutely uniform.

The first piece was always for the home, the next for the business. After that he cut a piece for each family member starting with himself as the oldest and working his way down to me. After my brother's children were born, I moved up the appropriate number of notches. But in those early days, when it was just us, I got the last piece. After each cut, Pop would carefully examine the bottom to look for the lucky coin. Whoever got the piece with the coin was promised good luck for the coming year. You'd have thought that Life itself depended on getting that coin. Everyone wanted it.

After the coin was discovered and awarded, we'd have a little snack and go to bed. The next day, when there were others with us, we'd cut another "pita" that included everyone. But the one we cut for just the family on New Year's Eve was the real one as far as I was concerned.

All through high school, no matter what other plans I may have made for New Year's Eve, I was always home by midnight in order to share that family tradition. I wasn't required to be. I just wouldn't miss it. None of us did.

During my first year of college, I visited an "older" woman (she was probably 24) who was babysitting on New Year's Eve. I had met her a few months before at our local recreation center and danced with her a time or two. She was not only attractive but she had the biggest, softest, most irresistible boobs my young eyes had ever seen. It was also rumored that she "put out." My own sexual organ had never been in anything but my hand up until then and I was anxious to see if it fit elsewhere . . . not that I had any experience with where "elsewhere" was.

When she invited me to visit her on New Year's Eve, I had only one thing in mind, assuming my mind had anything to do with it. A little before midnight I groped my way inside her bra and got hold of that beautiful flesh. That, in and of itself, was nearly enough to ring my chimes. Then, with the subtlety and finesse of meat cleaver, I tried to force myself into her while she was in a sitting position on the floor, still wearing all her clothes. Take a moment and try to see that picture. After pushing her panties to the side and when I was in the neighborhood of her crotch, not even sure I'd made contact with anything, I blew my nuts and smiled a triumphant smile, thinking I'd just gotten laid. The only thing that kept this experience from being a comprehensive insult to her was my not asking if it was good for her too. And then to compound the insult, my eighteen-year-old cock didn't care that it had just gone off. It was ready to try again almost immediately. After another few minutes, I was ready for my second sexual experience with another human being, if the wildest imagination could call it that. With equal agility and sensitivity as before, I tried to cram my way into her again. I shudder to think how thoughtless and selfish and clumsy I was, thinking only about trying to get inside that warm, wet place before it was too late. This time I had only slightly more success before exploding another load. No sooner had I dropped this second wad than I was dressed and on my way home to spend New Year's Eve gambling and laughing with the family. In my mind, I had lost my virginity on New Year's Eve which only added to the holiday's mystique for me, however humiliating it was in retrospect.

The Club was already rocking by the time we arrived. It was slightly after midnight and the atmosphere was charged. As was my custom, I walked with him through separating doors into the strip club with which The Club was connected and into the office where he stored his vinyl and cd cases, which I would then help carry to his dj booth. This was an added bonus to any evening at The Club because there were always dancers sliding down poles or writhing in front of a ringside customer as we passed by. Lap dances were performed in a slightly less public area.

As soon as my DJ friend took over, the charged atmosphere became a super nova, as if everyone in the place was a mini explosion waiting to happen. I had a territory which I more or less claimed whenever I was in The Club. It was on the stage, right in front of the little swinging door that was access to the dj booth. From there I could scan virtually the entire room, watching the various styles of individual dancers. It was impossible not to move in some way to the steady, rocking beat and I found myself bobbing in a controlled way to the rhythm. The hypnotic beat sent me into a reverie and my mind wandered back to previous New Year's Eves. Since those early family days, it seemed as though I was never in the same place in consecutive years again.

There was one New Year's Eve I recalled in New York. I was married to my first wife at the time. We had been invited to an East Side affair at the home of Caroline, an old college friend. She had married a rather interesting man named Lou. Lou was an Ivy League type, very buttoned down, very soft-spoken and seemingly gentle. He had been raised by his mother after his father had run out on them. We all love our mothers. But Lou made this filial relationship the cornerstone of his life, much to Caroline's dismay. She had always been discreet when talking about Lou's relationship with his mother, but it was clear from reading between the lines that there was something, let's say, unusual about it and, as a result, him. On the only occasion when I even mentioned the word "mother" in his presence I read volumes in his silent expression. At the mention of the word "father" Lou turned crimson. No one spoke that word in the presence of this otherwise erudite and cultured man.

Another couple whom we knew had also attended the party at Caroline's and both women had a report to make about Lou's behavior during the night. I was oblivious to what had been going on, but it seems that at a certain point, when Lou was well into his cups, he danced with both my wife and the other female friend. Without any warning, Lou brought each of these women's hands up to his mouth and bit down on their fingers with such force that there was still a mark when they discussed it several hours later. They each said that he got this other worldly expression on his face, as if possessed, and then smiled as he crunched down. Needless to say, Lou had a rather bizarre and creepy side which only manifested itself on special occasions.

Caroline and I drifted apart as time passed. Lou was not keen for her to maintain friendships, however harmless, with any other men. I later heard that she suffered considerable abuse, both physical and psychological, at his hands and the marriage eventually failed. He's the only biter I'd ever heard of up until then. Now, of course, nothing surprises me.

One year, while serving in the Counterintelligence Corps of the US Army, I found myself in Vienna for New Year's Eve. I'd like to say that I attended one of those traditional gala performances of *Die Fledermaus* but that's not the case. There was an opera story connected with that Viennese New Year's Eve but it was Puccini.

I had visited Vienna the previous October. It was my first real look at another country and culture. Until then I never wanted to stray more than a day's drive from my Ohio home-town. I went into a panic over the idea of being stationed in Germany and spent the first three months as close to my footlocker as possible. But there was obviously some kind of wanderlust and sense of adventure lying dormant in my soul because it wasn't long before I wondered what was around the next corner or over the next hill.

It took me no time to adjust to the notion of having a leisurely coffee and pastry at a Viennese café, reading several newspapers and watching the world go by. I found my way to the Weiner Statsoper and bought a ticket for a performance of *Tosca*, my favorite opera.

The title role was sung in German while the tenor sang in Italian. Because I understood neither, I wasn't concerned one way or the other. But I sensed that something was not right between these two singers. I was in a box that was close enough to the stage that I could see what appeared to me to be some hostility. My mind was filled with theatrical intrigue and monumental egos clashing. At the end of the opera, on cue, Mario fell to the stage and Tosca admonished him to get up. Of course he didn't and she threw herself from the top of Castel St. Angelo. The curtain dropped and the applause was enthusiastic. Tosca came out for a curtain call but there was no tenor to be seen. She went back behind the curtain until the audience demanded that she return again. She did, joined by Scarpia, but still there was no Cavaradossi. Next curtain call those two and the conductor emerged from behind the curtain. My imagination contrived this great feud, whereby the Italian tenor refused to be seen with this German bitch. I clung to that notion from October until the New Year's Eve in question.

Somehow I got myself invited to the American Embassy. I have no idea how this took place but there I was, dressed like a regular person even though I held the Army rank of a private first class. It was the first of countless times when I'd be the only person I knew in a room full of people. I must have engaged someone in conversation, probably whoever invited me, and had a dance or two, probably had a glass of champagne and toasted the New Year with all the others. But the thing that made the evening memorable was a conversation I had with an American woman about the performance of *Tosca* in October. It turns out that she had also been there that night.

Contrary to my romantic notion of some great rivalry between the stars, this woman told me that it was reported in the papers the next day that when Cavaradossi's "mock execution" took place and he fell to the floor of the stage, the poor tenor conked his head and was out cold. While Tosca and Scarpia were taking curtain calls, people were trying to revive their unconscious colleague. I liked my version better.

My DJ friend had the place in a frenzy. Every available space seemed to be taken and people were dancing where they stood. My glance swung in a about a 170 degree arc, taking in most of the room. In front of me was a lovely, round, brown woman I had met previously. She was from the Solomon Islands. Our eyes met for an instant and she smiled her huge, open smile and pointed a finger at me. I acknowledged her with a smile and pointed back at her. Located where I was, people often thought I had some official capacity. That and the fact that I never moved from there the entire night could easily have created that impression.

As I scanned the room, I was aware of a number of individual dancers. One was on the dance floor, slightly to my right. She was wearing a shimmering, dark, backless dress and shoes that had three-inch platform soles and six-inch spiked heels. The dress clung to her with a kind of desperation that suggested it needed her more than she needed it. How she was able to dance with such abandon in those shoes is one of the Life's mysteries. But dance she did. Another woman looked to be about 6'2" with long blond hair which made her even more imposing. She danced like a snake and most male eyes were one her at one time or another. Occasionally my eyes would focus briefly on a dark haired woman to my left. She wore a pair of jeans and a tube top. Her hair was on the frizzy side and she appeared to be dancing without thought or concern for anyone else, totally in her own world. As she shook her head from side to side, her eyes would take mine in for a millisecond, but without any noticeable acknowledgement at all.

An hour passed and, if anything, The Club got more crowded. Fists were pumping in the air when a new track came on. I wondered what this scene would look like without the music, all these gyrating, bobbing, E driven bodies burning enough energy to light the city of Los Angeles.

I had spent some memorable New Year's Eves in Los Angeles. I had even done a picture called **New Years Evil**, which took place entirely on New Year's Eve. It was the first starring role I had in a film, name above the title and everything. It didn't have much of a life at the time but has become something of cult classic since, which was of little consequence as far as I was concerned. Siskel and Ebert had declared it Dog of the Week. I wrote to them and insisted that they had underestimated the film considerably. I thought it should have at least been a candidate for Dog of the Year but they never responded.

I spent another New Year's Eve on the beach in Santa Monica. We watched the sunset, always a spectacular sight. But even more spectacular was the moonrise. It was a full moon and the second of the month, making it a blue moon as well. I was with a group of actor friends. These three women shared a house in Santa Monica which was a refuge and haven for members of their theatre company and friends. On regular occasions we'd kick in for food and the three of them would work with soup kitchen efficiency to feed us all. This Blue Moon New Year's Eve made that standard ritual just that much more special.

Another New Year's Eve, I went to Palm Springs with Phil the Horse, an actor I'd worked with in New York. We had both ended up in Southern California, he because he was from there, me because – well, just because. His mother had a condo in Palm Springs and since we had nothing better to do, we decided to spend the holiday there. He knew a few people there from previous visits but not well enough to be invited to any parties, so we bar hopped. The most significant thing that happened in Palm Springs was that I lost a lucky coin. Perhaps owing to that family tradition, I am in the habit of carrying a special coin. On this occasion it was an Eisenhower silver dollar that a woman had forced into my hand in Nashville when I was there for a Soap Opera Festival at Opryland. She came up to the stage, called my name and when I went to her, she put this silver dollar in my hand and closed my fist around it. She was a rather interesting looking woman to begin with, with dyed black hair in what looked like a 50's style, glasses with frames that were loaded with rhinestones and came to a point at either side. She looked like she was on the cusp of mystical and weird.

I started to say that I couldn't accept this coin from her when she looked deep into my eyes and said, "We give these only to the people we love." No one else received a coin from this woman, even though there were half-a-dozen of us from various soaps on the stage. It became my lucky coin.

I kept that coin in my left front pocket where all my lucky coins go. It was my second silver dollar lucky coin. The first had the date of my birth year and was worth a lot more than a dollar. I had to cash it in for phone money after I lost my wallet at the Ohio State Fair. My dad was angry because he had to drive twenty-five miles to pick me up and wouldn't give me a dollar so that I could reclaim mine from the druggist who was holding it for me.

It has always been my habit to make decisions by flipping my lucky coin. I reserve the option of not doing what the coin says, but mostly I go along with it. I figure it's as good a way to make decisions as any, particularly if I have no strong feelings one way or another.

I retraced my steps in Palm Springs to try to find the Eisenhower dollar but to no avail. Someone must have found it and decided it would bring them luck. I was only upset for a little while and then found a new coin to take that place of honor.

I noticed that the frizzy haired woman to my left shook her head in my direction with more regularity. These occasional glances allowed me to get a better look at her. She had a pretty face and was wearing no noticeable makeup, which means she probably had it applied with a subtlety that I was too dense to observe. I tried to place her ethnically without success. She could have been Greek, Italian, French or maybe Middle Eastern. Her hair was thick and about shoulder length. Her figure was trim and had some roundness to it without being voluptuous. She appeared to be about 5'7" until I noticed her shoes. They had two-inch soles and three-inch heels so she was probably closer to 5'4".

She continued to dance within herself, as it were, shooting occasional glances in my direction which I noticed only when I was looking in her direction. They were far too subtle to detect peripherally. I thought nothing of it because there was nothing unusual about her glances, nothing telling or provocative and they didn't last as long as a blink. Besides, like most men, I suppose, I wouldn't have thought any more about it any way. Women don't look at men the same way men look at women, not with that same unmistakable intensity and desire. And this particular man *never* gets it. I have spent my life thinking I was the ugly duckling and find it very difficult making the transition to swan. There has never been a shortage of attractive women who have found something interesting about me. I just never figured out why and, therefore, couldn't market it or take it seriously.

A similar thing happened in Los Angeles on still another New Year's Eve. As I indicated before, I often find myself in a party setting where I'm the only person I know. Somehow I had met this very wealthy woman from Texas who took a shine to me. There was nothing about her that I found physically attractive but she was a nice person and that was enough to accept her invitation to a New Year's Eve party that a friend of hers threw in a high rise on Wilshire Boulevard. In my mind I was merely escorting this nice, older woman to a party. The hostess was another rich Texan, single and bleached out. She was also younger and I might have found her attractive if she took more interest in herself. She needed to lose forty pounds or so and she sweated a lot. She was as close to a Texas caricature as I'd ever met personally, complete with "Eeeeeeee-Haaaaw!" She and Hank the Yank would have made a perfect couple.

At a certain point in the evening, the hostess took me aside and asked point blank, "Do you intend to fuck my friend?"

I was taken aback by the question itself as much as by its bluntness.

"No," I answered, "I have no intention of fucking anyone."

"Not even me?" she cooed.

"That's a little embarrassing," I answered. As sexually adventurous as I have been over time and as free a thinker as I am, I still have this shyness or insecurity or whatever that sometimes makes me seem like I just fell off a turnip truck. I'm not nearly as cool as I may appear.

"Honey, every woman in this room wants to fuck you. Pick one."

I later learned that both these women, and perhaps the others too, regularly engaged in swinging parties. This New Year's Eve party could have been one for all I knew. If so, it went completely over my head – as usual.

Something else happened at that party which I have never been able to explain. It has nothing to do with sex or the sexes. It had to do with the entertainment.

I don't know whether to call this guy a magician or a psychic or what. But at a certain point in the evening, he had the stage. He looked out into the room, searching for a pair of eyes, I suppose. He finally found mine.

"You, sir. Would you like to do a little experiment with me?" he asked. I returned his look with skepticism. "You don't have to do anything embarrassing, I promise."

"O.K.," I agreed.

"Now then," he continued, "I want you to think back to when you were getting ready to come to this party. I want you to see the change that was lying on your dresser or wherever you keep your change. Now I want you to, in your mind, see that change there. Don't put your hand in your pocket, just try to remember that change on your dresser. Think about it for a minute and try to remember how much money you had in change lying there. Try to see it in your mind."

At this point, he asked someone to hand me a piece of paper and a pen. "Write down how much change you think you have in your pocket now, the amount."

I thought and tried to picture the amount of change that was on the dresser and that I now had in my pocket. Finally I wrote down a figure, 87 cents. While I was concentrating on the money, he was concentrating on me, as if he were able to see my thoughts.

"Put that piece of paper in your left jacket pocket." I did.

"Now I'm going to write down a figure and I want you to put it in your right jacket pocket." He did and I did.

"Now," he said, "take the change out of your pants pocket and count it." I counted out $1.32.

"How much do you have?"

"I have exactly a dollar and thirty-two cents."

"Now read what you wrote down, the piece of paper in your left pocket."

"Eighty-seven cents."

"Now read the paper that I wrote on."

I took his piece of paper out of my pocket, knowing that I'd never seen this guy before in my life and hadn't even spoken to him at the party. There should have been a camera there to catch my expression. I was incredulous.

"What's it say?" he asked.

"I don't believe it," I answered. "It says a dollar thirty two."

Everyone applauded while I looked dazed. Throughout the rest of the evening people came up to me to find out if I was somehow in cahoots with this guy. I have a magician friend that I asked about it and he has no idea how the trick was done, assuming it was a trick. And if it wasn't a trick, what was it?

The frizzy haired one looked into my eyes in earnest. I looked back. That was apparently what she needed because the next moment she was standing next to me.

"I wonder why everyone tends to gather around the dj's booth?" she shouted into my ear. I shrugged and smiled. I could see how beautiful she was now. She had what I call a Libra face, perfectly balanced, so that if you covered one half and then the other, they would appear to be the same. Most people have two distinct halves of their face. If you doctored a photo and flip-flopped say the right side of their face so that it became the left side too, they'd look one way. If you were to do the same with the left side, it would look different again. For some reason, in my limited observation, Libra people tend to have two sides that more or less match. This is not scientific and probably has no merit but if I think it's true, it is to me.

Now that she was closer to me, she stayed where she was. She had entered my territory and seemed to lay claim to me. But she continued dancing, once again oblivious to the rest of the room, shaking her head from side to side as she'd done before, very much into the beat of the music.

The Club also featured a South African percussionist who did a couple of sets per night on congas. He was also a friend of the DJ's and mine. When he started his set, the already wild atmosphere became hysterical. His drumming and his appearance provided a tribal authenticity that was irresistible. All hands went into the air and you could hear the screams above the volume of the music.

Percussionist had a traditional attitude about women which permitted him to keep what he referred to as a stable of women available to him. Even though he was currently living with an Aussie woman, he felt it was his birthright to maintain sexual contact with as many others as either necessary or possible. At the moment, he was fascinated by what he referred to as "sushis," that is, any woman who had Asian looks.

Two sushis were dancing immediately in front of Percussionist and, therefore, in front of me, since I was standing next to him to his left. These two women obviously knew Percussionist and expended a great deal of energy trying to gain his attention. He remained aloof, smiling at each in turn, but maintaining his concentration on his drumming.

My dark haired beauty noticed these two women and pointed them out to me with a glance.

"It's a dance competition," I shouted into her ear. "The one who wins gets him as a prize."

"What?" she shouted, and put her hand on my face to draw my mouth nearer to her ear.

"I said they're having a dance competition. And he's first prize," I repeated.

She smiled an acknowledgment and continued dancing without moving any farther away. As she danced now, however, she made it clear that I was a part of her world. Our eyes met regularly and there was substance in our glances.

How does this happen? To my knowledge I had done nothing to attract this woman. I hadn't displayed my green and purple iridescent breast feathers. I hadn't strutted or postured the way the male of the species does. Yet, this attractive woman, who could have all the attention she wanted, seemed to have found me interesting. I don't wonder this out of vanity. I just wonder how Nature works. What is there about that initial moment between two people when they appear to know more about each other than reason could possibly suggest? No matter how many times it may happen in one's life, there is a freshness and mystery about it that defies any kind of explanation. It is totally organic and primitive. Every living creature has an attraction to another of its species that is absolutely fundamental. And even though I was not entirely aware of this phenomenon at the time, it was happening on this New Year's Eve with a woman I'd never laid eyes on before. As it tends to happen in Nature, she had somehow singled me out for a further look and I clearly had nothing to do with it beyond my mere presence.

"I love to watch other people dance." She cupped her hands around my ear as she shouted these words. "Some of them really like to put on a show."

"I know," I answered. And after a moment, "You don't seem to be dancing for anyone else's benefit."

"No, I dance because I like feeling the music. It wouldn't matter if anyone was around or not." As she spoke these words she put her arm around my shoulders.

I couldn't help being aware of the attention but as slow as I am, it didn't really register as anything more than natural. I was as comfortable standing there talking to her as if we'd known each other forever and were just out for a night on the town. There was nothing more to it. Whereas in some instances I tend to be rather shy, when there's nothing at stake I can talk to anyone anywhere anytime. This was one of those latter instances.

I began thinking about this particular New Year's Eve and the importance I had attached to it. I leaned toward her ear. "Do you find that you tend to attach any particular importance to New Year's Eves? Do you get more optimistic?"

"I'm always optimistic," she replied. I liked the answer. It's the answer I'd have given if someone had asked me the same question.

Who was this woman? There didn't appear to be anything cheap or easy about her. She wasn't even overtly sexy or provocative. There was nothing about her appearance that suggested anything that I could read. I've been around a lot of women and even though I don't necessarily know when they're interested in me, I can read behavior and body language in general. Nothing tipped me off about this mysterious person. She seemed very normal and friendly and open, no subtext.

In a little while she worked her way toward a man on the dance floor. He was around her age, give or take a couple of years. He was nicely dressed in a casual sort of way. His hair was longish and he had a pleasant face. He had her coloring, that is to say he looked Semitic or Mediterranean. I decided for some reason that he was probably Lebanese. They spoke to each other as if they were already well acquainted. Since nothing had registered with me anyhow and I had made no investment of any kind, I thought nothing of her wandering away from me.

After talking to him for a moment, she returned to my side. Again she put her arm around my shoulder and cupped her other hand around my ear. "That's my brother," she said. "I wish he'd find somebody."

We stood there in front of the dj booth watching the show unfolding before us. She was not actively dancing now but it was impossible for either of us to keep from moving. As we stood there, I was aware of our arms touching and then, from time to time, our hips. There was a suggestion of intimacy that felt so organic that it nearly passed without my noticing it.

Eventually the brother came to where we were. I couldn't hear their conversation but I could see it. His motions said, "I'm ready to leave. Are you coming?" Hers said, "No, I'm going to stay a while." His said something I couldn't decipher. She picked up her bag from the floor, took out two blue tickets and handed them to him. He left.

When she returned to me it was only a moment before she slid her arm around me and rested her hand on my butt, stroking it gently. I responded by putting my arm around her and holding her closer. Finally, I was prepared to accept the idea that this woman had made some kind of decision that included me. I was still dumbfounded by it, to tell the truth, but I was prepared to accept it.

What was most profound about it from my personal point of view was that I actually had allowed myself to think that I could care in any way, however superficially, about a woman. It had been more than two years since I considered thinking about touching another women, let alone having someone's hand on my butt. It was a truly life affirming moment for me. The fever was broken. The torch was out. My heart was my own again and didn't seem to be damaged beyond repair. It was an epiphany.

I didn't luxuriate in these thoughts at the time because I was very much in the moment, even though I didn't entirely understand it. All I was thinking at the time was how nice it felt to have a beautiful woman next to me, doing what women do when they are interested in a man. It was enough and very fulfilling. Anything else would be gravy.

I hardly had time to contemplate what could happen next. The brother reappeared and this time their conversation had a different look to it. When it concluded, she came back to me.

"I have to leave," she said.

I accepted the news without emotion. "Can I contact you?" I asked.

She thought for a moment, looked into my eyes and said, "No."

"Then Happy New Year," I said.

"Happy New Year," she answered. Then she kissed me almost on the mouth but not quite. I put my arms around her and she responded to my embrace with a passionate hug. We gripped each other and held each other in a way I will never forget. Then they left.

I remembered a time on a ferry in the Greek Islands. There was a woman with her husband and child on the boat. Without a word passing between us, this woman and I communicated everything a man and woman wish to communicate about desire. I read the passion on her face and I'm sure she read me equally as well. It was an instant in Life when nothing else exists except the energy flow between two animals, in this case, human animals.

I felt that same energy as I watched Nefertiti, as I decided to call her, walk away with her brother. I never expected to see her again but it didn't matter. She had done me a service in Life that no one had been able to do. She made me think there might be another woman in my life one day, if only for that moment. And that was worth everything.

TWO NIGHTS AT THE OPERA

This is probably too obvious to bother saying, but very interesting things can happen when we put ourselves out a little. In this book, the story *Just Say Yes* is a perfect example. When you make an adventure out of Life and proceed fearlessly, all kinds of things can happen.

Oddly enough, my friend Sally was a catalyst for this adventure too. She called me on a Monday to inform me that through a friend of a friend, she heard that they needed spear carriers for a Russian opera company which was coming to town as a part of the International Arts Festival. I thought about it for a moment. Did I really want to be a supernumerary in an opera, spear-carrier being a euphemism? On the one hand, the ego could paint such activities with a loser's brush. After all I had been a tv star in America and a proper ac-tor in my time. But on the other hand, there was that sense of adventure, of doing something I'd never done before and, with luck, finding something to write about afterwards. I don't have to tell you what decision I made since you are now reading.

The Kirov Opera Company was to arrive on Wednesday. A rehearsal was called for 4:30 in the afternoon. I was one of the first to arrive at the stage door of the Victorian Arts Centre. The lobby inside the stage door bustled with activity. As I'd never met the guy who hired me, I had no idea whom to look for so I just stood around like everyone else, after signing in and collecting the various tags and identification cards I'd need to move through the facility. As others arrived and began filling the lobby, some of them seemed to know each other and started chatting until it soon sounded more like a friendly pub than an arts venue. Before long the security people behind the desk had to shout everyone to silence so they could hear their telephones and do their jobs. The group swelled to about forty over the next ten or fifteen minutes. Our leader, a guy named Rick, hushed us to silence.

"Thank you all for coming. Before we show you around the Centre, show you your dressing room and give you an orientation, I do have an announcement. The Kirov Opera Company was supposed to arrive yesterday. However, they are in Vladavostok at this moment. They were originally scheduled to fly over Dubai and with the trouble in the Middle East, they've decided that would not be safe since they're on a charter rather than a commercial airline. They're trying to re-route themselves. That means flying over other sovereign airspace and that means getting other governments to allow them to do it. In other words, it's a little bit of a mess right now and we're hoping they'll be able to get here by tomorrow. We're still planning to do a performance tomorrow night as of now. That means you won't be required for the full amount of time today but we will need you to come in later tomorrow and be prepared to stay right through the performance. So instead of coming in at 10 in the morning and staying until 1 and coming back at 4, you'll now be required to be here at 3 and stay right through. There's no other way we can do this. I apologize if it's inconvenient for you but we've all got to be a bit flexible."

Next we had a safety and security chat and other mundane business and were escorted around the bowels of the theatre, the cafeteria, a huge rehearsal hall which we'd never see again because by the time we got into the action, we'd be on the stage itself, and eventually we found our way to a rather large dressing room.

The first real excitement was walking onto the stage of the theatre. The set was like a box with no front or top. There was nothing hanging, no colors, nothing to break the sterility of the gray inside of the box. Behind and around the set, the stage was immense. And even though the designated playing area was substantial, it was dwarfed by the space around it.

I walked down to the apron of the stage and looked into the orchestra pit. The chairs and music stands were arranged loosely, as if someone had just left them a moment before. Looking down filled my ears with sound, just imagining what would come from there the next night. I felt myself getting excited. I looked out into the auditorium and saw three tiers of red seats, the highest one looking miles away, but still creating a cocoon around where I stood. Every seat focused on where I was standing. An empty stage always fills me with a sense of anticipation and potential. I imagined applause coming from thousands of hands. The adventure was already worthwhile. I was standing in the middle of magic.

Back in the dressing room we were fitted with pants and tops which we were then responsible for hanging somewhere in the dressing room near our make-up tables. It was as much as we could do until the Russians arrived.

For them to do that took the intervention of both the Australian Prime Minister John Howard and Vladimir Putin, assuring governments that this was a legitimate arts enterprise and the charter plane was not going to drop any bombs while in their airspace.

Upon arriving at half-past two on Thursday, I learned that the Kirov Opera Company had only arrived one hour before. But they had agreed to do a performance that night anyway. What I later learned was that the Kirov Opera Company was paid per performance when they were on the road. The pay they received for each performance equaled a week's pay back home. I know performers. We'd do back to back shows for six years if we got a week's pay for each one. Russian performers were no different. I could just hear them saying, "Da! Da! Are you nuts? We're performing tonight! A gig's a gig and this one pays retail."

On the way to the dressing room, you could feel the excitement building. The buzz was an opening night buzz. Signs to the various wardrobe, make up and rehearsal rooms were in both English and Russian. Stagehands and others whom you passed in the hallway spoke Russian to one another. Almost no one spoke a word of English to anyone. It seemed like there was a climate of suspicion and distrust, very Slavic in its darkness. There were interpreters where they were needed but in general, it felt to me more like the cold war than glasnost or perestroika. Of course, what was no doubt happening was they were as panicked as anyone would be if they had to put on such a huge production in a few hours' time in a foreign country for a bunch of strangers. To be friendly and gregarious wouldn't be the first thing you'd think of in those circumstances. But I liked the drama of my interpretation better.

We had been taught the Russian equivalent of "G'day" the day before and were encouraged to use it with all the Russians except *Maestro*. Him you *didn't* say "G'day" to. In fact, we were instructed to say absolutely nothing whatsoever to him, not even look him in the eye. The Yank in me had a different sense of what's democratic and I blanched a little at the idea of treating that particular animal as being more equal than the others. But I kept it to myself and hoped I wouldn't run into *Maestro* and have my manners tested. I've since learned that it is SOP in the opera and classical music worlds. Nobody slaps Zubin Mehta on the back and says, "How's it going, mate?"

By now all the accoutrements had arrived and we were preparing for our one and only dress rehearsal, about an hour before curtain. Our costumes consisted of considerably more than we'd been led to believe the day before. First were the black tights. I'd never worn tights before and had to negotiate exactly how to go about it for a few minutes before attacking them in earnest, finally deciding to get my feet in first and ease them up, not try to pull them on like a pair of jeans. With the tights firmly hugging my feet and legs, I put on the black knee breeches with red spots and slipped on the matching top. Calf-length black boots added a touch. Then we each donned a metal breastplate and helmet and capped it all off with a black cape. We looked for all the world like Conquistadors from Hell.

Once we were all in our uniforms, we were lined up in the hallway, odd numbers pointed toward stage right and even numbers toward stage left. We must have looked like an interesting little army indeed standing one behind the other, waiting for the signal to move.

Suddenly Number One strode out toward the designated entrance. I was Number Three and followed quickly behind. I wanted to fall in step like a good soldier but figured that would be carrying the metaphor too far, opting to amble instead. Once backstage we were handed long sticks with what looked like a battleaxe on top. There must be a name for this weapon but as I'm not an authority on weapons of antiquity, I can't tell you what it is. It looked like a stick with a battleaxe on top to me.

Once we got our weapons we went to our respective doors, which were determined the day before. Obviously I was at Door Number Three. We were told that following a trumpet fanfare a light would go on just above our heads. That was the cue to open the door, step through and stand at attention with the spear standing at our upstage sides, arm extended. When the light came on, I pulled my door open and started to stride into position. I hadn't calculated the height of the door very well and the top of the spear stayed on the wrong side while I passed through it. I quickly recovered and made a note to myself.

On stage was chaos – intentional chaos. The cast was running to and fro, going through motions that must have meant something to them but looked like Bedlam to me. A largish woman sort of ran in my direction, sort of pantomiming some activity which meant nothing to me in the context of the rehearsal. In a few minutes the music climaxed and the curtain fell. That was our cue to leave the stage and close our individual doors.

Among the thirty or forty of us, only twenty were Conquistadors from Hell. The others comprised the backstage men's chorus. The singers tended to stay among themselves and the Conquistadors from Hell seemed to gather in small cliques. Since I didn't know anyone, had never done anything like this before, and tend to be a bit shy in unfamiliar environments, I pretty much observed only.

Back in the dressing room, I waited with the same kind of anticipation you'd have on any opening night, despite the fact that all I had to do was stand there like a mannequin. The time was approaching when we had to do our stuff. The other guys were pretty relaxed. I felt like I should be shining my breastplate or my boots or some other military thing to get ready for the parade.

Then Rick came in. "Line up, guys," he instructed. "This is what you're here for."

We took our places in the hallway and suddenly Number One was off. Down the hall we went, striding along on the plastic carpet which had been laid down to protect the real carpeting from the full body make up some of the cast were wearing.

I was handed my spear and took my position behind Door Number Three. There was a stagehand waiting for me, crouched down just to the right of the door. He looked up at me.

"I'll be opening your door for you, mate," he said. I was reassured by his Aussie accent.

"Thanks," I said and looked up to see that I was holding the spear low enough to get through the door.

The stagehand had his hand on the door handle, ready to pull it open. A light came on behind me, not the one overhead. I saw him flinch.

"Not yet," I whispered.

He hadn't been at rehearsal and didn't know it was the overhead light that was the cue. I breathed a sigh of relief when the door didn't open.

The stagehand then developed an interest in what was happening on stage. He was able to look through a crack in the set. He was absorbed in or maybe obsessed by what he saw. In any case, when the overhead light flashed on, he was still looking on stage.

"Now," I yelled. "Open the door!"

He jerked it open and I strode through, realizing immediately what had demanded his attention. Many of the people careening about the stage were stark naked. Some of them were young, round, Russian women. Their bodies were covered with a white make up giving them a ghostly look -- a very naked, ghostly look -- the only contrast being the dark, vertical line of pubic hair.

My job was to remain rigidly at attention and look straight ahead. I assumed the position but knew that no one would be able to see my eyes. So I looked from one gorgeous Russian body to the next, comparing sizes and shapes and generally feeling like I had suddenly become a Conquistador in Heaven rather than a Conquistador from Hell. No wonder the Aussie stagehand nearly blew my entrance.

While I was enjoying my spear carrying experience at an undreamed of level, the heavy-ish woman who had drifted my way during rehearsal returned, this time wearing a nun's habit. As I had no idea what was actually supposed to be happening on stage, I was unprepared for everything. I weigh about 72 kilos. This nun outweighed me by at least 25 kilos, even though she was easily four inches shorter. Slavic nuns, it seems, carry a bit more heft.

When you're on stage, a good actor should be prepared for anything. I thought I was. But I wasn't. I was watching beautiful bodies. The nun apparently thought my stick with the battleaxe on top was a stripper's pole secured to the stage. She slung her entire weight onto it, grabbing it with both hands and swinging around and around, pulling me completely off balance and nearly pulling me over. I caught myself just in the nick of time and stabilized before losing my balance entirely and embarrassing – no make that humiliating – myself in front of a packed opening night houseful of Melbourne's elite. A moment or two later the curtain fell and I beat it off stage, closing Door Number Three behind me.

We could hear the applause all the way back to our dressing room. The Kirov Opera Company had triumphed. I got dressed quickly and left.

The next night, when we got to the dressing room, the war stories began. One guy announced that he was shocked and indignant and insulted by all that vulgar nudity on stage. He said that it was bad enough having to stand there, but at a certain point, a naked woman riding on a naked man's back, rose up and exposed herself right in front of him. One of the other guys yelled, "You weren't supposed to be looking," which got a big laugh from rest of the Conquistadors from Hell. Another guy hadn't calculated how tall the helmet made him and knocked it off when he stepped on stage. That got a laugh too.

But the best one was Number One. He also had a stagehand opening the door for him. When the light from behind came on, the stagehand jerked the door open. Number One wasn't paying attention to lights, so when he saw the door open, he strode through. He looked across the stage and saw no other Conquistadors from Hell. Out of his periphery he saw that there was no one beside him either. Quick thinking saved him. He immediately pulled down his stick with the battleaxe on top and assumed a menacing stance, looking from one side to the other as if looking for some culprits. When he saw none, he went back through his door and re-entered to the stage a second time when the overhead light came on.

There was less of a sense of urgency on this second night. Whereas before everyone was dressed and ready hours before, this night there was a much more casual feel, like that of seasoned veterans before a battle. Practically no one had all his gear on. You'd see one guy with his breeches and tights on and a Hard Rock tee shirt. Another had tights, the helmet and sneakers. One young man who caught my eye was sitting in a corner alone. A small orchestral score was open in front of him on his dressing table. He held a baton in his hand and was obviously conducting the piece of music in front of him. He was in such an intense state of concentration that you could almost hear the music yourself. Certainly he was hearing it. He'd look up every now and then, imagining the various sections of the orchestra and cuing them to come in stronger or softer with his expressive hands. I wished I knew what the piece of music was so that I could enjoy it with him.

Rick came in and got everyone focused. "O.K., guys, it's time to line up," he announced.

I took my place with a steely determination not to be caught off guard or off balance this time. I would be the Rock of Gibraltar. I would be a giant redwood. I would be immovable. If the flying nun wanted to whip around on my stick this time, she could swing and yank to her heart's content. I would be ready for her.

In position behind Door Number Three, I greeted the stagehand, checked to make sure I could clear the door and waited. When the light came on behind me, my guy didn't flinch. He held the handle firmly with a tension that was ready to activate his muscles. He glanced out to the stage but it didn't hold his attention like before. The overhead light came on and he jerked my door open. I strode out. Instead of planting my feet together as I had been instructed, I widened my stance, planting that stick onto the stage as if it would stand on its own. While I was alert for the Slavic nun, I also allowed myself to enjoy the rest of the scenery. Beautiful, ghostly bodies were flying around all over the place once again.

One of them came right at me. This one was unbelievably round and firm and voluptuous. No one had done that the previous night so I was unprepared. She came directly at me and just before colliding with me, veered to my right slightly and jumped up onto a steel bar that was above my head. She was almost on my right shoulder, all of her gorgeous, naked self.

Then. Bang! The Slavic nun hit me broadside. She attacked my stick with a vengeance, flailing herself around as she sunk toward the floor. She yanked it this way and that as if trying to wrench it from my hands. I held firm. *Spin around on somebody else's stick, honey*, I thought. *This one ain't moving*. After a very long time she stopped struggling and came to rest on my foot. It might have just been me, but it seemed like she was trying to pull me over. Without that open stance, I'd have lost my balance for sure, particularly since my attention was elsewhere. The curtain fell and I yanked my foot out from under her. The naked one was still hanging on the bar above me, looking down and smiling as I left the stage.

After that, everything was an anti-climax. Everyone was in a hurry to strip out of their costumes and leave the opera world behind for a while at least. As sometimes happens in a situation like this, even the people who knew each other scattered like dandelion pods.

I was in no particular hurry to leave since I had no place in particular to go. This had been such an intense experience and represented an entire world for the past two days that to leave it suddenly would be like going cold turkey. The shock of the great expanse of reality outside these safe walls was a bit confronting. And if not confronting, at least a sudden and, for the moment, unwelcome change. Little by little I weaned myself, handed in my costume, pulled on a pair of jeans and a tee shirt and left this Russian womb.

Once I was on the street, I could still feel the remains of the adrenalin rush from the performance. I passed the Spiegel Tent. I hesitated for a moment. Some of my fellow Conquistadors from Hell would certainly be in there winding down. I don't know how long I stood there before I finally strolled on, away from the lights and into the quiet of the night, knowing that I didn't have to do anything like that again . . . ever.

THE ARCHIBALD

I had a graphic designer friend, the one who created the poster for my one-man show, **The Mark Twain You Don't Know**. He lived in the only apartment building on this particular street in Toorak. One weekend he told me to come over because the block he lived on was having a closed party. All the rest of the residences on the street were gorgeous houses. It was Toorak, after all. I didn't know what a big deal it was until someone compared it to Beverly Hills for me. Then I got it.

All the people who lived there had tables set up in front of their homes with drinks and goodies for everyone to share. It was beautiful day and the atmosphere was very festive and lively. Kids were running in the street and having their own parties. As is often the case in my life, I was an outsider. I was there by accident, or serendipity, or some other inexplicable phenomenon. As a result, I pretty much stayed to myself, watched the others and waited to see what might unfold. A few people nodded and said hi. They had to be wondering who I was and what I was doing there, but no one made me feel uncomfortable or unwelcome. They must have decided that if I was there, I belonged there. My friend was busy talking with his neighbors. That was fine with me. I just watched.

I was standing with a glass of red in my hand when this woman came straight at me and barged into my space with a purpose. She was dressed in what I'd call expensive casual and had a big smile on her face. She didn't mince words. "You have got a great face," she said.

Good opening, I thought. "Thanks." I didn't know what else to say. I've been familiar with my face all my life and while I recognize that it's exclusively mine, I don't think much more about it. Everybody has one.

"Has anyone ever painted you?" she asked.

I wasn't expecting that. "Nope," I finally said

"Why not?"

"Because nobody ever asked," I said.

"Well, I'm asking," she smiled.

That's how I met Dooley. And that was the beginning of a journey that eventually resulted in my portrait being submitted for the Archibald prize.

But it was a journey of unpredictable twists and turns. I soon learned that she and her husband owned a chain of schemata stores in Melbourne and she was also an accomplished artist.

Dooley invited me to come to her studio for some photos and sketching a couple of days later. She was focused and concentrated on her work but we had a lot of laughs along the way. She decided she'd do the portrait with me standing, leaning against a building. It was very casual and, I thought, captured my general attitude perfectly. Then, a couple of weeks later, she asked me to come by again. I saw the huge canvas that she'd put my leaning self on and I'd be lying if I didn't say I thought it was cool. She had another little canvas that just had my face on it that she'd done as an exercise. That was it. I didn't hear from her again for a long time.

When I did hear from Dooley again, I found out what had kept her so busy. It wasn't the schemata business. She was having an exhibition of a series of new paintings she'd done and asked me if I'd like to come along. The entire gallery was filled with at least twenty enormous canvases, all in her unique, liquid style. It was brilliant and colorful and, as it turns out, successful. She pretty much sold out. That allowed her to get back into her Archibald groove.

She asked me to come to the studio for Take Two. The large canvas with me leaning was nowhere to be seen, but the little face was still there. She made some more sketches and we talked about Life. She seemed a little upset, so I asked her what was bothering her. She told me that she and her husband wanted to get married by a rabbi. But because she was Jewish and he wasn't, they couldn't find a rabbi in Australia who would perform the ceremony. They had been legally married for years, had two children and grandchildren by then. But this one thing made it feel unfinished. "Are you looking for a rabbi that will marry you? Is that it?" I asked.

She said yes. I said, "I can take care of that. No problem."

Now, let's put Dooley on hold for a minute. I lived in Hollywood right before coming to Australia to live. I met Delta when I sang some kids songs at a park in Beverly Hills. Her daughter was in a kids' chorus that also performed that day. Delta recognized me from **All My Children**, a daytime soap I had been on in New York before moving to Hollywood. I noticed her sort of circling me for a while before she approached me. When she finally did, she told me that she would like me to sing some of my kids' songs for senior citizens at her synagogue. *That's thinking outside the box,* I thought. It turns out that her husband, Bro, was the rabbi. That was the beginning of a friendship that endures to this day. Delta and Bro have been to Oz at least twice. We met another time in London, when I took the Eurostar from Paris to meet them for lunch. And I see them every time I go back to the States. When I lived there, I often went to services at their synagogue in Pacific Palisades on a Friday night, even though I'm not Jewish. The congregation began asking if Bro and I were related. So, we told them we were brothers but had different parents. Henceforth, we were Bro to one another. The congregation he led was one of the more liberal forms of Judaism, Reconstructionism. Bro had written any number of books about interfaith marriages and bringing up interfaith children. So, when Dooley told me about her dilemma and I said I could handle it, I wasn't boasting. I was merely stating fact.

I contacted Bro and told him Dooley's problem. He told me to put her in touch with him. So, Dooley, her husband and their family went to L.A. a few months later. Bro converted Dooley's husband to Judaism, per his request. He said he had always felt Jewish anyway. Then, Bro married them. This cemented my friendship with Dooley. I had merely been a go-between but what I was able to do, no one else had done for them. In the Jewish tradition, what I did is known as a mitzvah. The Wizard of Oz might have called me "a good deed doer," and someone else might say it was a blessing, but under the circumstances, I prefer mitzvah.

So, fade out, fade in. More time passed. There wasn't much movement on the Archibald front but it didn't matter to me. I was busy with other projects and Dooley was busy with her paintings and the business she ran with her now Jewish husband. We would talk from time to time just to stay in touch.

A lot more time passed, during which we had no contact at all. Usually, she would have called me by now, but nothing. I finally decided to give Dooley a call to see how she was going. When she answered, she didn't sound like her usual, upbeat self. "Hey, Dooley. Haven't heard from you in a while. How you doing?" There was a long pause on the other end of the phone. Then she said, "I guess you haven't heard."

"Heard what?" She and her husband had been in a terrible automobile accident. Her husband was killed. She was pretty badly mangled and had been healing for the several months since we last talked, recovering from multiple surgeries.

I tried to say something reassuring but what can you say? Tragedy is a part of Life. We all know that on some level. Dealing with it is the thing. And only she could do that. All any of the rest of us could do was try to be supportive. But, anyone who knows her, knows that Dooley is a woman of enormous strength and character and indomitable spirit. She'd get through it.

And sure enough, after a few more months of rehab, she got the paint brush back in her hand. The first thing she did was a huge show dedicated to her late husband, depicting stories about him and their time together. She needed to do that. The work was stunning. The meanings were powerful.

I was sitting in a café in Malvern one morning when someone came up behind me and gave me a kiss on the cheek. It was Dooley. I had only spoken to her, not seen her. She looked wonderful and her smile was back.

Not long after that, she invited me to a small show they were having at her studio on a Sunday afternoon. You couldn't help but notice that she had difficulty going up and down stairs but she treated it like an inconvenience. A few weeks after that we caught up in that same café in Malvern. By now, we were back in the habit of calling each other and keeping in touch.

Then, one Saturday, my phone rang. It was Dooley. All she said was, "It's time." The next day I sat in her studio and watched while she made magic on a large canvas. I had never observed or experienced anything like this before, watching something emerge from a blank canvas. We chatted a little, but mostly I watched. I saw my eyes begin to materialize on the canvas. We were looking at each other but our looks were entirely different. I looked at her as I would anyone I was talking to. She looked at me in a way I've never been looked at before. It was intense and specific. She wasn't looking at me so much as looking at bits of me with this amazing focus. After a couple of hours, she was tired. "That'll get me started," she said.

Several weeks passed before I saw her again. I was at the same café in Malvern when Dooley walked in. She came straight to my table. "I'm sick of looking at you," she smiled. "You're all I've been looking at since that Sunday. I think about you morning, noon and night. I'm sick of you." She laughed. I asked her how it was coming along. "It's nearly finished," she said. "I'm going to take it to the framer next week. You want to see it before I send it to the Archibald committee?"

"Duh".

She took a photo of me standing next to my huge, blue face. The eyes that I'd seen materialize several weeks before at her studio were riveting. They were also undeniably mine. I couldn't have been more chuffed if someone handed me an Oscar.

She said she'd give me the painting after the judging was done. But in spite of my vanity and the thrill of having a portrait of myself, I just couldn't imagine that big canvas in my little apartment, so I said no thanks. So did the Archibald people, by the way. But Dooley got it to a boutique gallery in Sydney and someone bought it. So, now my face is hanging in some stranger's house, reminding someone of a lost relative that I seem to have resembled, a renaissance Dooley is painting again and I got another story.

THE FIGHT WITH RAY MARTIN

On the 8th of March 1971, Ray Martin, the Aussie legend, was the ABC's representative at the first Ali – Frazier heavyweight championship fight at Madison Square Garden in New York. In his autobiography, Ray describes the weigh-in ceremonies. And here I'll quote him. *There were rhinestone-beaded maxi coats, mink hats, spangles and chains and jewellery and alligator patent-leather high heeled boots. And that was just the black dudes. There were voluptuous women in evening gowns, spilling breasts and bling at midday.* Then he goes on to say, *That night 22,000 frenzied fans filled Madison Square Garden…Everybody from Barbra Streisand to Frank Sinatra turned up…Old Blue Eyes had even been registered as a Life magazine photographer so he could sit in the front row.*

Let it be known that I'm not interested in having an argument with an Aussie as esteemed and respected as Ray Martin. I'm not stupid. However, he's wrong about one thing. Frank Sinatra was the official photographer for Life magazine. That much is true. But he didn't sit in the front row. He sat at ringside. And the way he got to sit at ringside as the official Life magazine photographer is because he gave Burt Lancaster singing lessons when Burt was about to do a music theatre production of **Knickerbocker Holiday** in San Francisco. Burt Lancaster had been hired to provide color commentary for this fight. Sinatra knew this and his quid pro quo for the singing lessons was to sit next to him at ringside. The only officially designated spot that wasn't spoken for at ringside was the photographer's. That's how Sinatra became the official photographer for Life magazine.

How do I know this? Strap in. Because I'm about to take you on an amazing ride.

To put it generously, I was between jobs in New York. The official excuse was that my position had been eliminated from Channel 5. My position had been a producer. The truth was that the program director and I didn't like each other and he had the power to do something about it. But I often went to Channel 5 at lunchtime to play a nerf basketball game in the art department with my buddy, Syd, the art director at Channel 5. On this one particular day, two of our former colleagues from Channel 5, Art Fisher and Neal Marshall, showed up to talk to Syd about the graphics for a huge gig they'd landed in Hollywood: the first Ali – Frazier fight at Madison Square Garden. Art and I had done the first **Harlem Cultural Festival** telecast together and taken a trip to Puerto Rico with our girlfriends. I hadn't seen Art or Neal since they went big time. But I had no hesitation about telling them that if there was anything I could do in order to see the fight, just let me know. I fixed the odds at slim and none, but it was worth a try. Then I forgot about it.

A couple of days later, much to my surprise, I got a call from a guy who identified himself as a production assistant without identifying the production. "Can you be at the St. Regis hotel tomorrow afternoon for a production meeting at Burt Lancaster's suite?"

"Production meeting for what? I asked. "Who is this?"

"My name's Josh and I'm working with Art and Neal on the Ali-Frazier fight," he said. "And Art asked me to call you to see if you could come to a production meeting tomorrow?"

"The Ali - Frazier fight? At the Garden?" I was incredulous.

"Yeah," he said, sounding a little impatient.

"Yeah, tell Art I'll check my schedule and see if I can work it in," I laughed. "What time again?"

That's how I got hired as associate producer of the first Ali-Frazier fight at Madison Square Garden in New York City, the biggest, televised, global sporting event in history up until that time. It ain't always what you know . . .

Next day I hotfooted it to the St. Regis and up to Burt Lancaster's suite. I sat there at that production meeting like I knew what I was doing. I had no idea. I didn't know why I was there. But Art and Neal didn't hesitate to introduce me as their associate producer to Burt Lancaster and Archie Moore. Archie had been the light heavyweight champ in his day and, along with Burt, was doing color commentary for the telecast. As the meeting was winding down, Burt asked Archie something about throwing a jab. Archie stood up and motioned for Burt to join him. They were standing, poised as if they were going to get it on. Then Archie demonstrated how to throw a left jab. Burt mimicked him and Archie said, "No, no, man. You gotta twist it when you throw it so it snaps. Like this." He did it in slow motion until we all got the hang of it. Even I learned how to throw a jab. I haven't had occasion to put it to the test, but I know how if I need to.

When the meeting wrapped and we were on our way out, Art told me to show up at the Garden at 7 o'clock in the morning, then we all said goodbye. I still had no idea what I was supposed to do -- and to be honest, I didn't really care. I was going to get paid to be at what was to be known and billed as **The Fight**. Some called it the greatest fight of the century. As I walked to my apartment after the meeting, I thought about how this stuff seems to happen to me. Some random, serendipitous moment launches me into an adventure beyond my imagination. It has to be sheer luck, otherwise it's too weird to consider.

I got to the Garden before 7 o'clock. Who could sleep in on a day like this? Madison Square Garden was a shell, just one big cavernous, empty space. The remote truck was in the bowels somewhere and easy to find. Art was already there as was Stan, his AD. We had all worked at Channel 5 and were old friends, very comfortable with each other. I asked Art what he wanted me to do and his answer was, "Just hang loose. When I need you, I'll send Josh to find you."

I wandered into the arena. It was unrecognizable, just a huge empty arena. It could have been anywhere. Then, little by little, the workers arrived and began bringing it to life. Piece by piece, they brought in large what looked like blocks and wooden parts and canvas and padding and ropes and poles and put them all around the center of the ground floor, then went to work. After they were all fitted together, like magic, there was a boxing ring, ready for action. The huge center light was then lowered into its place. After that, they began hauling in seats and attached them to each other and to the floor until they filled the entire ground floor from ringside all the way back. Another group were doing the same thing in the upper tiers. As I watched this awesome transformation, Josh came looking for me. Art wanted me back in the remote truck.

What's up? I asked.

"We want to get some footage from the dressing rooms. Once we're live, we don't know how much time we'll have to fill before the fighters come out. If they decide to fuck around and play chicken to see who enters the arena first, we have to be ready," Art said. "So Josh'll take you to where the film crews are and you can pick up a cameraman and a sound guy and go to Frazier's dressing room and shoot some film."

"What kind of film?" I asked.

"Whatever," Art said. "You're a producer. Get something interesting."

I started off. "Wait," Art said, "you'd better put on your official jacket so nobody wonders what you're doing there. Nobody's allowed in."

Everyone involved with **The Fight**, whether on the television side or the film side, was given a jacket with **The Fight** on the back. Ours were yellow and the film guys' were green. Josh led me to where I could get my film crew and off we went.

My guys got set up in an area that would be unobtrusive and we waited. Before long some men came into the dressing room who looked like handlers of some kind. Nobody very important looking. Then there was some commotion that suggested something or someone important *was* arriving. When they entered the dressing room, I heard someone say, "There's Frazier."

I looked around at this newest group, trying to find someone that looked like a heavyweight champion. Finally I noticed a guy with a green robe on. *Must be him*, I thought. He wasn't much taller than I was, so I was surprised to learn that it was, in fact, Smokin' Joe. As soon as he walked into the dressing room, he spotted the camera and the sound guy. He and all the rest of us knew this wasn't an authorized visit and he immediately got pissed off. "Who are these motherfuckers?" he snarled.

I stepped out to where he could see me in my official yellow **The Fight** jacket. "We're with the tv production crew," I said, as authoritatively as I could. Before I could say another word, Frazier said, "Git these motherfuckers out of here! Ain't nobody s'posed to be in here."

I found a guy who looked like he had some pull and whispered to him that we had to get some footage in the dressing room and we'd be out of there as soon as we got it. He went to Frazier and whispered something to him. Frazier looked at me and he didn't look very friendly, but he sort of nodded without changing his expression. We got our footage and got the fuck out of Dodge.

In the meantime, Art had sent Stan to Ali's dressing room where he did the same thing. We never had a chance to compare notes about our receptions, but his couldn't have been as interesting as mine. When we both returned to the remote truck, Art sent Stan to a place away from the Garden to edit the two films. When I asked him what I should do, he told me to hang loose again and if and when he needed me, he'd send Josh.

I went back into the arena. By now it looked like Madison Square Garden for real. While I was admiring it and trying to project what it would be like in a couple of hours, from way up above, in the top tier of the Garden, I heard someone yelling at the top of his lungs. I couldn't tell who it was or what he was saying at first. Then, I could. It was Ali. He was walking all around that top tier of the arena, shouting the whole time nonstop about how he was going to beat Frazier because he's so ugly and how Frazier was no match for him and on and on. He continued shouting and walking as if he were trying to fill the place with his energy, his vibe. It was an amazing performance. Then he left. About half-an-hour later, he was back at it, walking around and shouting until he should have been hoarse. But he wasn't. He was pumping his self up.

It was late in the afternoon when Josh found me and said Art wanted me. It was approaching crunch time and he needed Stan in the remote truck. He asked me to go to where Stan was editing the film footage and send him back. And he said that if Stan wasn't finished editing the footage that I should do it and come back as soon as I could.

It was on the cusp of late afternoon and early evening by the time I got back to the Garden with the film. I delivered the edited footage and asked Art what I should do next. They were still worried that the fighter's would play games before the fight, so Art told me to go to ringside and wait. He wanted me to spot celebrities and other famous people as they arrived and see where they were sitting in case I had to ask them if they'd mind being on standby for an interview with Burt Lancaster before the fight. So, I went to ringside and watched and waited.

Now it was approaching fight time! The place was practically filled and the stragglers were pouring in as fast as they could. The Garden was coming alive with an energy that you'd have to be dead not to feel. All the people Ray Martin had mentioned, including the *voluptuous women in evening gowns, spilling breasts* were there, with their escorts who rivalled them in bling. Over there was Gene Kelly. Over there was Barbra Streisand. Over there were the all of the Apollo astronauts. There was Miles Davis. There was Woody Allen. I could have blindfolded myself and thrown a rock in any direction and hit someone famous. I wouldn't have any trouble getting anyone to talk with Burt. Right behind me, Jerry Perenchio, the guy who was the promoter of the fight and therefore my employer, was sitting with Diana Ross. Because I had my official jacket on, no one seemed to mind.

The broadcast team got into place. Don Dunphy was doing the blow by blow. He was a legend in boxing lore, considered by many to be one of the greatest play by play announcers in all of sports history. He called heavyweight fights going all the way back to when Joe Louis fought Billy Conn in 1941. Burt Lancaster and Archie Moore took their places. Archie was next to Don Dunphy and Burt was to his left next to the corner. Then Frank Sinatra came in to take his place at the corner next to Burt. He had a guy with him who -- let's put it this way -- he looked like he could handle himself in a pinch. He was carrying a large bag which I was later to discover was filled with loaded cameras.

As far as I could tell, nobody knew yet when the fighters were coming in, so since my job was to find people for Burt, I didn't think I should move. My yellow jacket was the only thing that saved me. I looked like I belonged wherever I was. I was aware that the time was approaching when something *had* to happen. You could feel the excitement building and the noise increasing and the next thing I knew, there was this tremendous roar like an explosion of thousands of voices screaming and shouting. I froze. Two undefeated heavyweight champions were making their way from their dressing rooms down their respective aisles and toward the ring -- where I was standing. There wasn't an open seat anywhere near me – obviously. I was stuck. I suppose I could have tried to quickly scoot up the aisle and disappear, but there wasn't a chance in the world I'd do that. I was standing between the apron of the ring and the first row of spectators. *Pfft. Yeah, right. Disappear, my ass.* So I just squatted down where I was, behind Frank Sinatra and Burt Lancaster and in front of Jerry Perenchio and Diana Ross And that's where I watched the entire fight from. No one in Madison Square Garden or any place on planet Earth saw that fight better than I did, except maybe the referee.

When you're squatted down on your haunches like that watching one of the greatest and most celebrated prize fights of a lifetime, it's possible -- or maybe I should say impossible not to -- tense up your leg muscles. Three minutes in that position, in the midst of all that excitement, felt like torture, but under the circumstances, I would endure it. However, I did have to stand up between rounds just to stretch out my legs and walk around a little bit. Because I had my official yellow **The Fight** jacket on, the people at ringside could have thought I was security, I don't know. All I know is no one said anything. After the first couple of rounds, Jerry Perenchio and Diana Ross started kibitzing with me between rounds. We were on a first name basis by the end of the fight. Another thing was the ongoing discussion and sometime argument I had with Sinatra. During the fight he was clicking away, trying to live up to his title of official photographer at ringside. (*You can Google the results. A Frazier left hook was on the cover of Life Magazine*). The guy with the bag of cameras couldn't have seen five minutes of the fight. He was busy taking the camera Sinatra had just zipped through with one hand and handing him a new, loaded one with the other. Sinatra had to snap his fingers a couple of times because he thought they guy was too slow. Between rounds, when I wasn't chatting with Jerry and Diana, Frank would turn to me and say something like, "Frazier is kicking Ali's butt, isn't he?" And I'd say something like, "Bullshit! Look at Frazier's face. Ali's ripping him apart!" The words changed as the fight progressed but not our relative points of view.

The fight, itself, lived up to all its hype. Both men took a hell of a beating. Ali jabbed and danced and landed punch after punch until by the later rounds, Frazier's face looked to me like raw meat. Frazier, in turn, bobbed and weaved, taking Ali's punches and punishing Ali's body as he kept moving forward relentlessly, waiting for a chance to throw his lethal left hook. He never backed up once. Ali even did a rope-a-dope at one point and just let Frazier pound away. They were obviously both ready for this contest. In the 11th round, Frazier finally landed a left hook and staggered Ali, but he recovered. Then, in the 15th and final round, in the far corner from where I was, Frazier hit Ali with a vicious left hook that the referee later said *was as hard as a man can be hit*. It knocked Ali on his butt and he still got up in three seconds. However, it was enough to swing the decision in Frazier's favor. Sinatra shot me a *told you so* look and I just shrugged my shoulders.

There was a rumor going around before the fight that the management of the Garden and all the New York fight officials wanted Frazier to win, that he'd been given preferential treatment from the beginning, a better dressing room, etc. So, when Ali went down, that sealed it. I don't know if that's true or not, but that's what was being said.

When the fight was over and the Garden cleared out, the electricity in there was still palpable. You didn't know what to do with yourself. I went back to the remote truck for a few minutes just to say thanks and goodbye. Art and Neal were elated, as you might expect. They had pulled off the biggest televised sporting event in the world without a hitch. When I left the truck, I still didn't want to leave the Garden. It felt like this was the entire world and it had just stopped cold.

I'll give Ray Martin the last word. He said, *Even from 20 rows back each punch resonated with me like someone smashing a leather lounge with a baseball bat. Frazier won the fight, yet he was admitted to hospital for three days with a face so puffed and out of shape that it looked like he was suffering from a bad case of the mumps. Ali secretly visited a hospital, afraid that his jaw had been broken. It hadn't; it was just badly bent.*

So, that's a longwinded way to tell you why I knew where Sinatra sat. Hope you enjoyed it. And by the way, if you know Ray Martin, ask him to give me a call if he'd like to reminisce. We're probably the only two people in Australia who were at Madison Square Garden that night.

THE GREAT GATSBY

At around 3 in the afternoon on a gorgeous, 24-degree day, the 24th of April in 2025, Faline, Butch and I sat in three white outdoor chairs looking out across the vast gardens and grounds of one of Melbourne's landmark estates. We had had a picnic earlier at another location on the estate, which consisted of classic French sandwiches of *jambon et fromage* on a baguette. Mine was made by the artist hands of Faline, who is French and confirmed its authenticity. These were accompanied by almond croissants from two of our favorite Melbourne bakeries, a variety of cheeses, all French, of course, and a chilled red. After this sumptuous feast and a little stretch-out in the beautiful sunshine, looking up past a tall narrow palm tree at two puffs of white clouds against the brilliant blue of the Australian sky, we decided to have a stroll around the estate. What neither Butch nor I knew at the time was the serendipity of us being there at this moment. **The Great Gatsby** was published in April, 1925. April 2025 was the book's 100th anniversary. We were essentially on a pilgrimage without knowing it. This is where my friendship with Butch began. As we strolled around this estate, Butch and I were remembering where certain scenes had been played. Faline took a photo of us standing where we'd played our . . . Wait. You know what? I probably ought to start at the beginning.

* * *

Two years after I came to Australia to live, my marriage went south. Or maybe it went north since I was now in the Southern Hemisphere. In any case, it was over and I had decisions to make.

I had had some success as the writer and composer with a musical, **Nothing to Wear** at the Victorian Arts Centre, but I've never been someone who is satisfied with doing just one creative thing. I've always had a need or compulsion or tendency – whatever it was – to do lots of different things. My creative quiver contained a number of arrows and I liked shooting them all. It's probably fair to say that I've been a jack of many trades, but never mastered any one of them. And I have always been okay with that. In that regard, variety has definitely been the spice of my life in virtually any context you can name.

I had been in a play with a couple of guys I met through my ex. I honestly didn't think I'd be doing much acting in Oz and did that as a lark. Then, through a playwright I'd met through my ex, I was asked to play an 80-something-year-old Comanche in a play he'd written that was being put on at LaMama. I liked the synchronicity of having done a play at the original LaMama in New York and then doing one at LaMama in Melbourne, so I said yes. I had an absolute blast playing that part. First of all, there wouldn't be a chance in the world that I'd ever have been able to play a Native American character in the US. And besides that, it was a rich character with lots of possibilities. Since no one knew me to begin with, I was able to hide inside old Comanche Joe and Chris Wallace completely disappeared.

It wasn't long after that that I was approached by Bicks, who had been told about my performance by someone at LaMama. Bicks was functioning as a casting director for an outdoor production of **The Great Gatsby** that he was also in. There was one role they were desperate to fill and so far, nobody stood out. I met with Bicks but don't remember if I even auditioned. Nevertheless, I ended up being cast as Meyer Wolfsheim, the Jewish racketeer who was Gatsby's mentor. We opened on the 27th of December 1997. Remember the 27th of December. You'll see it again before we leave each other.

* * *

Okay, let me pause for a second. That production was a watershed moment in my life in Oz. I can trace almost everybody and everything that happened to me subsequently back to that show. Many of the stories that make up this book are also linked to that show. It was like a meteorite that splashed into the ocean and started a Gatsby tsunami.

Butch is my oldest friend in Australia. He played Gatsby. He has gone on to unimagined heights as an actor, both here and in Hollywood. Butch and I have seen each other through some of our hardest challenges as our friendship unfolded. I knew all of his women and he knew all of mine. I

133

knew all of his problems and he knew all of mine. We have had a lot of laughs and shed a lot of tears through the years since then. The last time I ever was drunk was one year on my birthday when Butch bought me my first . . . and second . . . and maybe third Guinness pint. I did Ecstasy for the first time at his suggestion. I was a fixture at all of his and his friend's parties. I remember one time when a young woman came up to me and told me how cool it was that someone my age would be partying with that crowd. I looked at her and smiled, "I'm not the one that's new here." Butch and I took a trip up to Port Douglas and Cape Tribulation together. And later, a trip to Paris. Until Butch introduced me to his agent in Melbourne, who agreed to represent me, I was represented by an agent in Sydney. I could write a book about Butch, and it would be a good one. But if I did, it would have to be a tell-all and, frankly, it's no one else's business. I'm not social media. And besides, this is about **Gatsby**. On with the tsunami.

Sally and two of her classmates at the National Theatre were extras on **Gatsby**. Sally features in two other stories, *Just Say Yes* and *Two Nights at the Opera*. She later made sure I was cast in a play she was doing with a theatre company she was a member of. And that play was directed by TiDi, who has since become one of my close friends. I gave her little boy classic rubber replicas of the 7 Dwarfs that I had played with as a child. I met the guy I called Nugget in *The St. Valentine's Day Nugget* story through his niece, another of the extras on **Gatsby**, like Sally, a student at the National Theatre.

School Boy was 19-years-old and still at uni when he became assistant director of **Gatsby**. He had been involved with another show at this Victorian estate the year before. For the last two weeks of rehearsal, he became our default director. He was in the production office when the producer and the vanishing director had a screaming match one day. The producer said the show was too long and was way over budget. The vanishing director still wanted to add scenes. The air was blue. The director had a nervous breakdown or a tantrum or the vapors or some equally Victorian malady and vanished. Okay, that may be a little harsh, but clearly, he wasn't there for the last two weeks of rehearsal. We never saw him again. So, when School Boy became our director, his instruction to the actors was to keep doing what we were doing. School Boy went on to have an acting career on several long-running television series and is a successful podcaster. I have never missed his birthday and even went to Byron Bay for his 40th, where I sang him a special birthday song. He's happily married to a film director (who cast me in a commercial) and has a lovely daughter.

Red had a role in **Gatsby**. She and I often talked about spiritual matters between scenes. It was Red who invited me to the artists' retreat referenced in *Just Say Yes* on the Mornington Peninsula, and then another in India. I met Sushi, Lydia and Beta at the one in Oz. In India, I met a Brazilian woman that I had a subsequent thing with and spent two unforgettable months in Brazil. In another book, **The Palindrome Adventure**, I write about visiting Beta in Berlin and Lydia in Nairobi. I have gone to Mumbai twice to visit Sushi and her family. I've participated in events she organized at her Indian Classical Dance Academy. We are still in touch and regard one another as brother and sister.

Maddy, who was one of the organizers of the Mornington retreat became one of my closest friends until we had a falling out based on a misunderstanding, one of my few regrets in Life. It was through Maddy that I met a couple in the Dandenongs, Jinx and Timmy, that I have virtually become family with. Together they created an Arts Academy that continues to thrive. Timmy also cast me in a beautiful piece of cinematic art that he created. I can't just call it a movie. That's way too ordinary a description for this work. They also created an international children's film festival that is still going. They met The Perfesser through me and he became a judge at the festival.

Through Butch, via my agent, I met one of my very closest Aussie friends, Alphabet. It turns out that when he was a journalist, he reviewed the play I did at LaMama. He also interviewed Butch at that time. Our friendship came later. It seemed like whenever Alphabet and I talked, especially when I was feeling creatively frustrated, he would suggest solution. And it always worked. I won't go into the details because each of them is *a-whole-nother-story*. Suffice it to say, he was another of the major waves from the **Gatsby** tsunami. The last wave is The Perfesser.

I didn't know this at the time, but The Perfesser is an Australian icon. He had been involved in the Australian film industry virtually from its inception. Okay, maybe not from its inception, but certainly from its heyday in the 70s. He was an actor, wrote film critiques, doctored scripts, taught subjects related to film writing at several institutions, and with a colleague, reviewed movies on the radio for years. All I knew during **Gatsby** was that I had a scene at the top of the show and he had one at the bottom. In the middle we had a lot of time to talk – a lot of time. And talk we did. Boy, did we ever! I started going to movies alone when I was 8 or 9. I'd see three at the Strand and two at the Star virtually every week until I was a teenager. After that, maybe only one or two a week. He may not have started that early, but he more than made up for it. When **Gatsby** finally closed, it seemed that The Perfesser and I hadn't finished talking yet. It should also be said at this point that he could be – let's say – rather rigid in his opinions about film or most anything else, for that matter. I say opinions, but what I really mean is categorical pronouncements. I like a good "intellectual discussion" myself, therefore we often were at loggerheads over movies.

So, after **Gatsby** ended, he and I felt a need to continue arguing – I mean, discussing intellectually – movies and other matters, but mostly movies. Before he moved to rural Victoria, we got together fairly often for a coffee or to watch a movie at my place. I have a huge library of films. Whenever we were deadlocked on a movie, he'd introduce some obscure Japanese or French or Lithuanian or Tongan film to make an irrefutable point. I claimed that he hadn't seen a mainstream film since 1980. When we talked about directors and I might mention John Huston or Francis Coppola, he'd pull Kon Ichikawa out of his ass and say, "Now, *this* is a director". He was a tough adversary.

After he moved to rural Victoria, we saw less of each other, but still kept in touch by phone. Every now and then, he'd get permission from The Committee, as we referred to his partner, to take the train into Melbourne and pop in for a movie session. On the phone one day I had mentioned a western that I was especially fond of, *The Big Country*. He couldn't shit on that movie fast enough. It was one of the few films he had seen back in the day and thought it was garbage. I told him he should re-visit it. So the next time he came into the Big Smoke, I forced him to watch *The Big Country*. I wish I'd recorded his reaction because it could be one of the few, if not the only time, he changed his opinion and he declared it much better than he'd remembered. That could have been my only clear-cut victory.

He, The Committee and I went to see some plays at LaMama and would have a bite afterwards. It was then that I got to know The Committee as a sharp-as-a-tack, equally opinionated adversary. She wouldn't let you get away with anything. I now understood why he always deferred to her for permission to come to my house and play. They were a perfect couple.

As the years passed and our friendship grew, one day I decided to tell him my age. Up until then, I never divulged that information because first, it was not anyone's business; and second, because while it wasn't an issue for me, it could have been for potential employers. But during our chat that day, he made some outrageous reference to something that suggested he knew more about whatever it was on account of his age and experience. When I told him I was two months younger than he was, he nearly choked. From that time on, our friendship deepened even more.

The time came when his health was beginning to be an issue. In his youth, he had been active in sports, mainly cricket, but those days were long gone and he didn't move around enough to keep all the parts functioning properly. His feet began bothering him, then aching, then he lost feeling in them and his movements were greatly limited. I jumped on a train to visit a few times to hang out with him and those occasions were always a joy no matter how he felt.

I met his children whenever they came down to Melbourne. I went to an ACMI event that honored him. I had to go on crutches owing to a bicycle accident, but I went. I got him representation with my agent when he needed it. We were mates. We were buddies.

When we talked on the phone one day, he began telling me that he was having trouble remembering things and went to see someone about it. He was diagnosed with the beginnings of Alzheimer's. It got so our conversations were less frequent, but I always called him on his birthday and holidays. One year I left a birthday message on his answering machine and a few days later, he called me back. He said The Committee had to remind him who I was. We had our last real conversation that day. I'd still call from time to time and leave messages, but never got a reply. One day I received an email that was allegedly from him. As I hadn't been able to contact him in so long, I was suspicious. I called our agent and asked if they could enlighten me. They told me he was now in a facility and had been completely consumed by the hideous disease that took away the one thing that was as important to him as anything else he ever had: his memory.

All of the above came from one theatrical production.

* * *

Now it's time to spend a minute on the production of **The Great Gatsby** itself. First of all, it dragged the audience from one location to the next on an estate that covered seven hectares. Those forced marches extended the already too long production to unimaginable lengths. After a little while, as the plot snailed its way along, audience members figured they'd had their picnic, saw some theatre in the lovely night air but it was getting chilly and enough is enough until at the end, there wouldn't have been enough audience left to fill a broom closet. Each scene was someplace else, so the audience had to pick up all their things and move to where Tony, who played Nick Carraway, narrated the set-up for the next scene. Scott Fitzgerald would have been embarrassed. This script definitely needed a lot of editing!

There were also gratuitous scenes added for "flavor," making the show even longer. One was when Gatsby and Nick Carraway had a nude swim in the estate's lovely pool, while the audience stood around the edges. You can read **_The Great Gatsby_** a thousand times in every language on earth and you'll never find a scene where those two characters go swimming in the nude.

The Great Gatsby was Butch's favorite book. He could quote from it at the drop of a hat. So, when auditions were called for this production, he just had to give it a go. When he went in for his first audition, the vanishing director let him know in no uncertain terms that he wasn't the first choice, that they were actually trying to get Guy Pierce for the role of Gatsby. The fact that Guy Pierce had no interest in this production didn't seem to register.

Bicks told me that he brought Butch in for callback after callback, only to be rejected by the vanishing director, saying, "No one was quite right, not quite what I'm looking for." Bicks was confident that Butch was the guy and asked the vanishing director to see him yet again. The vanishing director was waiting for someone to blow him away. After this one, the vanishing director was still unconvinced. The list of potential Gatsbys had shrunk to a handful of total unknowns. Bicks brought Butch a final time. This time, after the audition, Bicks put pressure on. The show was opening in a three weeks and the lead wasn't cast. The vanishing director finally said okay.

By this time, Butch's potential dream role was turning into a nightmare. When he finally joined the cast, very late in the rehearsal period, he was just taken from one location to another and told to "stand here" and deliver his lines. That was the extent of his direction. Okay, that's not quite true. Before he vanished, the director did manage to shout out, "I don't believe you" at Butch from time to time. This reached its most unhelpful extreme one day when in the scene, Gatsby looks at his watch and says, "It's ten past two." The director shouted out, "I DON'T BELIEVE YOU!" at the top of his lungs. Butch cocked his head to the side, put his hands on his hips and said, "I looked at my watch and said it's ten past two. Which bit don't you believe?"

It was at this point when he learned he was doing the nude scene at the pool. He called our agent and said he wanted out. Our agent was in the business of getting people jobs, not getting them out of jobs. Essentially, he said, "Suck it up." One of Butch's concerns was a "guy thing" that can best be described as a George Costanza shrinkage moment. Gatsby and Nick Carraway were supposed to "frolic" in the pool, then get out and perform a scene buck naked. After several performances, they were resigned to it and decided to have some fun. They accidentally-on-purpose splashed water onto the audience members who were crowded around the edge.

Then, a new wrinkle – no pun intended – was introduced. Originally, our vanishing director had thought a nude swimming scene would be a good marketing ploy to draw in the gay crowd. But it backfired spectacularly. The book was on the school curriculum that year and was, therefore, required reading. Many schools arranged field trips to our production. High school students being what they are, some found ways to enhance the experience. Word got out of the gay-induced nude scene. After the first of the high school students saw the show, word spread city-wide and from then on, "tomorrow's leaders" showed up with laser pointers and focused them on the penises of the actors when they emerged from the pool – night after night after night . . . accompanied by a storm of muffled giggles.

One night, toward the end of our run, Butch had another "interesting" moment. If you don't know the story, Gatsby is shot at the end and actually *does* fall into the pool . . . clothed. It was rigged so that Butch would fall onto this little raft and it sank slightly but not enough so that he couldn't breathe. After that climactic moment, the remaining audience was moved to the last location where The Perfesser had his scene. At this point, School Boy would go to the pool and tell Butch it was okay to get out. On this one night, there was an audience member who stayed by the pool and didn't seem to care where the rest of the audience went. School Boy waited and waited for the man to leave. Butch was face down on his raft, wondering where School Boy was, and if it was safe to come out of the water. Finally, Butch heard School Boy ask the man if he needed anything. The man said, "No." Then he called down to Butch, "Hey, what do you want to do after the play?" It was Butch's dad.

Another gratuitous scene was when Bicks jumped into the pool fully dressed in formalwear because he was on fire. Try to find *that* one in the book. There was a big 1920s party scene in the ballroom of the estate. The vanishing director decided he wanted someone to jump in the pool and asked for volunteers. No one was interested until Bicks raised his hand. He was game for anything, so he decided it would be more effective if he *had* to jump in the pool. He decided that in a drunken state, he'd accidentally catch fire and jump into the pool to put it out. He decided to tuck a red paper napkin into the top of his cummerbund leaving a huge un-missable red triangle down the front of his pants. He contrived to be in conversation with one of the female partygoers who had a long cigarette holder, which she was casually waving around as they chatted. At the right moment, Bicks turned his back to the audience and lit the napkin with a lighter, then turned around and rushed toward the pool with flames flying, screaming , "Oh my god, that woman just lit me on fire!" By the end of the run, he kept adding paper to make the flames bigger in order to enhance the effect, timing it just right, until it began to get a bit warmer each time. But, while Bicks wanted to create a spectacular effect, he wasn't stupid. So, he decided to put something on underneath to prevent any serious damage. He opted for a pair of Speedos. They'd hold everything in place and seem protective. It didn't come into his equation that Speedos are made of polyester and quite flammable. He only learned this back in the dressing room one night after he'd put in an extra bit of red paper and the flame turned out to be a conflagration. When he inspected the situation, he saw that the Speedos had melted, taking away most of his pubic hair with them.

* * *

This location was perfect for **Gatsby**. The set was the entire Victorian estate, stables and all. The costumes were absolutely first class. The party scene in the ballroom rivaled anything the movies could produce. It was spectacular. That was the only scene Sally and her two classmates were in. At that time, Sally was living in a share house with her cousin, which she remembers as party central. So, they partied all day, then met at the estate and got all dolled up in their 20s wardrobe for the party scene in **Gatsby**. But that wasn't the end of the ongoing party.

Sally's ex lived at the estate as some kind of caretaker while studying psychology. He had nothing to do with **Gatsby**, but that didn't keep the triumvirate of female actors from continuing to party long into the night after the final curtain. Butch and Sally both reminded me that I was there during one of the wild party nights. As the night wore on, some of their gang started to fade. At some point, she said, I announced loudly, "I'm not tired" in my American accent and they all cracked up. They were all 20 years or more younger than I was. Long after **Gatsby** finished, Sally said, "I'm not tired!" became a joke among them, all unbeknownst to me. The whole event was little more than a big party for Sally. In her actor's secret imagination, she thought she'd be a great Daisy, but kept it to herself. The truth is that she would have been.

* * *

One of the challenges of performing outdoors without mics and sound equipment was being heard. Projection is something you learn in acting school. Outside at night, projection became more like shouting. One of the characters was a really good-looking guy with a rich baritone voice. He must have missed that class because he turned into a high-pitched, screaming banshee whenever he was onstage. Intimacy was not a feature of our production.

In addition to his assistant directing responsibilities, School Boy took a small part in the show. He played a waiter who served Butch, Tony and me. The situation was Meyer Wolfsheim, Gatsby and Nick Carraway were having a drink. The waiter comes in and exits a few times. While he was coming and going, School Boy always did some kind of business that he hoped would crack Butch up. He tried and tried, but Butch knew what he was up to and never cracked. If he did, I don't remember it. After **Gatsby** ended, School Boy cast Butch and me in a student film he wrote and directed. We had a great time shooting it. Butch played a Russian boxer and I played his Russian trainer. We did accents and everything. One of School Boy's classmates was assigned to edit the film. Digital editing was far less sophisticated at that time. School Boy called one day to say that the editor had accidentally deleted everything. I happen to have saved a photo of one of the scenes. It is the only existing documentation of that wonderfully funny, intellectually stimulating, classic prototype of great acting and directing left from one of the most outstanding, potentially award-winning student films ever made. You'll have to take my word for that one. I later did another short film for School Boy in which I used an Aussie accent. This time the editor didn't lose it, but at a wrap party when we met, the editor was surprised to learn that my natural accent was Yank. He was sure I was a fair dinkum Aussie. Ask any Australian actor if anybody off the island continent can do an Aussie accent and they'll laugh in your face. To that I say, "Hah!"

* * *

We ran for several weeks and I don't remember ever being rained out. Audiences were always big and it was a profit share situation, which meant that each person's salary was predicated on a formula that gave each of us a pretty good stipend at the end. I made enough money for a trip to Greece and a little extra. It's fair to say that the show was a huge success.

As I was putting the finishing touches on this story, serendipity once again rose to the occasion. In one of those wonderful, rare moments in Life when things just happen as if by plan, Butch called me to tell me that he received this random message on his Instagram account: *A funny thing. I'm in Lisbon with my great friend So-and-So and I just realized I saw your performance in **The Great Gatsby** at The Estate in 1996. Wonderful show, small world.*

And to that, I say, Amen.

A

In all the stories I've told about various adventures I've had since moving to Australia, I have been conscientious about not revealing too much about my personal life. In most of them, I've been an interested observer or a narrator or a sometime participant, certainly affected somewhat, but not much else. All of that changes with this story. This adventure is life-changing, a story so unimaginable that I still shake my head in wonder at how it unfolded. And I should quickly add that this story is told from one perspective only . . . mine. It's how I see it and how I lived it. When I've quoted conversations, they are accurate to the best of my recollection. The rest is subjective, as only an emotional experience can be. But first, I have to go back to a bit in my personal history.

New York City is the only place I've ever *wanted* to be. That was where I was headed when I ended up in St. Louis selling Vicks Vaporub. All the time I was in St. Louis, I dreamed about being in New York. We'll leave the St. Louis adventure for another time. But other than that time in St. Louis, I've always been contented to be wherever I found myself and acclimated to my surroundings. I am where I am, full stop.

Before I finally went to New York to live, it held a special magic for me, like a wonderful dream, a fantasy. After I went there to live, it became a magical kingdom that I fit into like a hand in a glove. We were made for each other. My rhythm in the little Ohio town where I grew up, unbeknownst to me, was a New York rhythm. I went to New York for the first time on a high school senior trip. It scared the shit out of me, but it was a good kind of scared. I loved it. The book I'll write about those days already has a title, **Apple Sauce**. But again, that's another story, not this one.

Now, a little background on my Australian history. I mentioned my friend, Alphabet, in the **Gatsby** story. And I mentioned that he nearly always had the solution for my creative frustrations. For example, we were having one of our Summits, as we referred to our catch-ups, one day in Melbourne. I was stagnant creatively. As we chatted away, it came up that I had done some musical revues in Hollywood, which I facetiously titled **Greatest Hits**. Very few of the people who knew me from what we'll call the Gatsby Era on, also knew that I wrote songs. My musical, **Nothing to Wear**, at the Victorian

Arts Centre, was a pre-Gatsby event. So as Alphabet and I talked that day, he said the magic words, which were to become prophetic forever after, viz. *You know what you should do?*

That particular "what I should do" was to put on a cabaret show, essentially a musical revue, at The Butterfly Club in Melbourne, mimicking what I'd done in Hollywood. I didn't know there was such a place. Fade out, fade in. I did four shows at The Butterfly Club over the next few years. The first was titled, **Greatest Hits**, as a nod to the original Hollywood show. The second was titled **Tall Poppy Blues**, the title song of which is one of my funniest songs, if I do say so myself. The Butterfly Club later took **Tall Poppy Blues** to the Melbourne Fringe Festival. The third was **Les Femmes**, my personal favorite, in which all the performers and musicians (except me) -- were brilliantly talented women. It was subsequently selected for the Melbourne Cabaret Festival. And the final one was titled **Story & Song**, a one-man show in which I told the story of how a song came to be written, then showed a video of a performance of it. Thank you, Alphabet.

At another Summit, when I was once again creatively frustrated . . . wait. I'll get to that in a minute. First, I'll tell about the third You know what you should do. I had been involved with a couple of guys who were trying to produce a television series about a moment in Australian history. It's a much longer and far more interesting story than I'm going to go into now. Suffice it to say that my involvement with this piece of Aussie history was substantial, to the point that when they ran out of options, they asked me to write a four-part television treatment for them. This was after they had exhausted all the funds they raised to date without making a deal and I had already done a hell of a lot of work for free. As I got into the treatment, though, I thought it would be fair if I got some kind of credit. I asked for a "story by" credit -- no money -- just a "story by" credit. They demurred and as a result, my participation ended. The project ended for them at that point, to the best of my knowledge. Alphabet lived through the unfairness and the frustration with me and commiserated until eventually he said the magic words: *You know what you should do.*

The result was a book I wrote titled **The Dreaming Team**, a true story about the first Australian cricket team to play at the home of cricket, Lords, in England. The team was all Aboriginal and it took place at a time when Australia was a British colony in the 1860s. It's a great yarn, in case you're interested.

Now, back to the second of Alphabet's suggestions. Sitting in the café, during this particular Summit, he suggested that I do a podcast. He knew I had a multitude of stories about my life before Oz, in New York, Hollywood and elsewhere, and thought it might keep me off the streets and creatively active, thus alleviating any potential frustration before it could take hold. Hence, **The Chris Wallace Chronicles** were born. That was in 2019. It is now the 26th of November 2025 as I write these words. From the time he first suggested the podcast, I've produced 13 seasons of the **Chronicles**, ranging in subject matter from weed and Mark Twain and everything in between.

Okay, now for a little *more* background. After my first marriage ended, I met a woman at a function in New York. She was fun and beautiful and accomplished. She had a great laugh and a stunning smile. Her name began with the letter **A** and that's what I always called her: **A.** She grew up in East Harlem, which was then an Italian American neighborhood, but now is called Spanish Harlem. In addition to being fun and beautiful and accomplished, she was a tough, no bullshit, died-in-the-wool New Yorker. We hit if off immediately. This was in the 1960s.

As time passed, it was clear that we had something special. She moved into my Westside apartment with me. We took a trip to Puerto Rico with another couple. We had parties galore. One Christmas, she made and decorated our tree with clever caricatures of each of our guests, then gave them as gifts. She also planned a surprise birthday party for me. People started arriving: first a couple who lived on one of the floors above us. I thought they just happened to drop in. We always left the front door unlocked. Then more and more people kept arriving and the wine and food came out and the gifts. I was in shock. I couldn't believe that anyone would do something that thoughtful and loving for me. No one else ever had or ever has. One of the gifts she gave me was a wastebasket made by a Native American from buffalo hide. I still have it at my apartment in Melbourne. I also still wear a wide, leather belt she gave me. And hanging on my wall is a framed 45-rpm recording of a Christmas calypso song that I wrote, titled **The Baby Smile. A** gave me that too. (Alphabet used it in one of his television specials).

A and I spent a weekend in Amish country in Pennsylvania. And here I have to pause for a sec. We were taking a walk on this dark, country road near where we were staying. My tough, street-wise, East Harlem **A** was in Nature, not her usual habitat. This was the country. It could have been Mars to her. It was a typical, moonless, dark night in this farming country. She heard a noise that scared the shit out of her. I heard it too. It came from the side of the road where there was a fence. We were walking down the center of this deserted road because there was absolutely no traffic at this time in the evening. I started toward the sound to investigate. She grabbed my arm. She didn't want me to leave her alone in the middle of the road. I reassured her and said I'd be right back. There was no way she was going to stay there by herself, so she came with me and we approached the fence together. She jumped and screamed when she saw a shadow move on the other side of the fence. I saw that it was three or four cows and started laughing. She was still shitting herself. My big city girl, **A**.

Later on, when my mother decided she was going to take two of my brother's kids to Greece to meet the family there, **A** and I decided we'd go too. She had already bonded with my mother when we went back to Ohio for a visit. In fact, **A** was the only woman I was ever with that my mother took such a shine to. They stretched filo dough together for spanakopita, something that Mom had only ever done with my Pop previously. We visited Mom's family together in Alexandroupolis. Everyone loved **A** there too. My first cousin's little boy referred to her as "the good one". I had been there with my first wife a couple of years before. We also went to Turkey together, where my mother had grown up. She never called it anything but Constantinople, in spite of the fact that the Turks now called it Istanbul. We were in awe as Mom told us about her life in those days. One of the highlights was when she pointed up toward the Topkapi Palace and told us she used to hear the harem girls laughing when she was walking home from university. She took us to the bazaar where you could buy anything. I bought a Turkish drum and Mom helped **A** pick out a small Persian rug.

After that, **A** and I went to Delphi together, then to two of the Greek Islands, Hydra and Mikonos. Mykonos must have made an impression on me because I remembered one day when this young American woman came out of the post office waving an envelope at her Greek boyfriend saying, "I got it, baby." That scene stayed with me and when we got back to New York, it became the catalyst for my first novel that I titled, **Mykonos**. I began writing it soon after we got home. I'd never imagined writing anything of consequence before that. If I'd had the imagination or the perspective, I could have concluded that **A** was my muse, but I didn't.

I've spent a lot of time trying to analyze my behavior after that. It wasn't until recently that I got what may be a handle on it. I was humiliated that my marriage ended in divorce. Neither my brother nor my sister got divorced. Only me. As much as I cared for **A** and as much as my family loved her and thought she was the one I should be married to, I never considered it. She and I never talked about it either. It wasn't on either of our radars. And quite apart from that, up until that time, I had always been insecure about women. I honestly couldn't figure out why any of them would want to have anything to do with me. I always thought of myself as a Greek misfit in a small Ohio town, despite my academic successes and the fact that I was elected to president of a thousand high school organizations. I never thought anything I did was something that everyone else couldn't also do just as easily Let's just put it this way, my self esteem was none existent. In college, for instance, I was on a committee for something or other that met at one of the sorority houses. One of the other committee members was a lovely Scandinavian woman named Ingrid. Once a year, there was what was called a Sadie Hawkins Day dawn dance to which women invited men. I had never been invited. Ingrid invited me. My reaction was to feel sorry for her because she couldn't find anyone better to invite. I turned her down. She was the homecoming Queen. That was typical behavior for me. I was all show and no go.

Another thing that I've been mulling over recently is that when I was a kid, my mother was never at home with me. Because of the restaurant, we never had a home life. Christmas and New Year's were the only holidays we celebrated as a family, the only time we were all at home together. I never felt a mother's love the way most people did. When you're a kid, whatever your life is is what you think is normal. Mom worked at the restaurant. My older sister looked after me in the evenings, but she was never tender with me . It's easy to conclude that I craved female attention and tenderness, but felt unworthy of it because I hadn't received it from the primary source, my mother. I protected myself by putting up a wall. I could be charming and fun and flirt and dance all night, but never close the deal in any way. I tried to go steady one time in high school. It was an unmitigated disaster. When I became an adult, after my Pop died, my mother and I became great friends. It was almost as if, after a year of grieving, she was suddenly free to be herself. One day when she was visiting me in Hollywood, she confessed that she had always felt enormous guilt for having abandoned me. You could see the pain in her eyes. When my brother and sister were kids, she was at home with them. With me, it was different. My conclusion is that it must have left a hole in me that I spent the rest of my life trying to fill in any way possible. Thus, beneath the surface, I was extremely insecure and tentative around women while secretly craving their attention.

My insecurity went through a metamorphosis when I was married. My first wife had several very attractive friends that she must have talked to about me. Women are people too, you know. Whatever she said must have piqued their curiosity because more than one decided to investigate their friend's spouse for themselves. Without much effort, several decided to seduce me and succeeded. And seduce is a carefully chosen word. I was a pushover. That was the first time somebody of the opposite sex was paying unsolicited attention that even my dimwitted, insecure self could understand. Until then, I had assumed I was an ugly duckling. The occasional conquests I may have experienced always seemed accidental, as if the woman in question had a lapse of judgment and just happened to pick me or was stuck with me. But my wife's best friends turned me from an ugly duckling into a fucking swan. Literally. That's probably too delicate. They brought out the dormant dog or, even more accurately, the horny goat in me. In any case, when that marriage ended in my humiliation, I compensated by allowing myself to be "noticed". I was feeling my oats and as much as I cared for **A**, I didn't feel a necessity to be faithful to her. I confessed cheating on her with a really random woman whose main attraction was store-bought boobs. Somehow we survived that, but **A** didn't forget it. Then one day, she saw a phone number on my desk that belonged to one of her classmates in an NYU night course. I had gone to one of her classes with her and this woman either gave me her number voluntarily or I asked for it, I don't remember which. I never acted on it, but I had it. When **A** discovered it, that was the final straw. All the time we were together on the Westside, she had kept her apartment on the Eastside. She moved back into it. Who could blame her? What confident, intelligent, self-respecting, independent woman wouldn't? I was an asshole, pure and simple.

One of my friends from the NBC Page staff was going out with the woman who had sublet **A**'s Eastside apartment. She and **A** were now roommates. My Page buddy fixed **A** up with one of his colleagues at NBC news. When I learned of it, I did what every asshole does: I just *had* to have her back. I was a cliché. I even went to see a shrink, something I'd never considered before or since. I was hurting . . . bad . . . and deserved to. Somehow I convinced her to come back to the Westside for a night and we made love. After that, I didn't see her again until one day some time later, when I had re-married and she was married and pushing a baby carriage. We said hello and goodbye.

That was fifty years ago, give or take. During those fifty years, my life blossomed into a creative adventure. I produced big shows on television, like **The Harlem Cultural Festival**. I produced **New York: A Great Place to Live**, the kick-off event of New York City's Diamond Jubilee at Lincoln Center and **Uptown Sunday Afternoon** at the famous Apollo Theatre in Harlem. I became an actor and was in the ensemble of the number one soap opera in America, **All My Children**. I wrote, narrated and wrote the musical score for a wildlife film, **In the Balance**, which won the Silver Award at the New York International Film and Television Festival. I sang one of my songs, **A Special Thing to Be**, at a Soap Opera Festival in Nashville at Opryland. I did all kinds of things, any one of which would have been amazing. Taken together, they have provided me with enough copy for several memoirs. And I haven't even mentioned them all here!

After that I went to Hollywood and had a career in television and movies. I was elected to the Board of Directors of **Screen Actors Guild**. It was there that my song-writing career blossomed. I created **Greatest Hits** that played several venues in Hollywood, like Carlos 'n' Charlie's and The Backlot. I was invited to put the show on at Georgia Frontieri's home in Bel Air (she owned the Los Angeles Rams football team) and Casey Kasem invited me to his Christmas party. I produced a fund-raiser in Santa Monica for the Clinton - Gore ticket in 1992. I was flying high.

Then I came to Australia without a thought of what it may have in store for me. I've already mentioned a couple of things, but add to that a fund-raiser I produced at the Victorian Arts Centre, **A Helping Hand**, for Quadriplegic Hand Foundation. I worked in a ton of Aussie television series: **Blue Heelers, Stingers**, you name it. I created a one-man show, **The Mark Twain You Don't Know**, which toured Victoria, Adelaide and Sydney, and which I then took to Hollywood and New York City. Through all that, I had been married three times, the last of which brought me to Oz and none of which lasted very long. Add them all up and you won't get ten years.

Then one day, about fifteen years or so ago, the former NBC Page friend who had introduced **A** to her husband somehow found me through a clipping about one of my shows at The Butterfly Club in Melbourne. He was now retired from NBC News and living in Boston. We began corresponding by email. He brought me up to date on a number of people we both knew. One of the things he told me was that **A**'s husband had passed away. Her email address was among the emails he sent me and I decided to offer my condolences. I have never been one to stay friends, or for that matter, stay in touch with any of my former partners, wives or lovers. It's just not something I do. I move on. But for some reason, I reached out to **A**. She responded graciously and added something about my mother. She had returned to Istanbul and thought of Mom, referring to Mom as her "almost mother-in-law", then said that being called **A** in my email touched her.

After a couple of years had passed, one day **A** flashed through my mind. Maybe I was putting on the belt she gave me, I don't know. Anyway I thought I'd write and see how she was doing. I wrote to the last email address I had. No response. I didn't give it another thought.

I have since learned that during those same fifty-some years, **A** was having an equally full, adventurous life. Because her husband was in the news business, he was assigned to various bureaus where news was happening across the world. They lived in Japan and Jordan and Germany and Italy over the course of time. They had two daughters, the older one of whom was in the baby carriage when I saw **A** for the last time. Because they were living overseas, they had ample time and the resources to do a lot of additional traveling. Holidays took them to Ireland and Scotland, to Kenya and Eastern Europe, to the Alps and probably other places that I don't know about. The girls were educated overseas and were automatically multi-lingual by the time they all returned to the United States, settling in New Jersey.

Another thing I couldn't know was that after some years passed, her two daughters tried to interest her in dating sites since she was still a viable, attractive woman, but she couldn't be bothered. It just wasn't her thing. After a little more time had passed, something did interest her. She was working a memoir so her family would know about her life before them. The memoir included our time together on 77th Street. She had no idea what I had done or was doing or where I was or whether I was alive or dead. She decided to try a Google search, but it turned up too many Chris Wallaces for her to filter through and she gave up. More time passed.

Then, on the 18th of June this year (2025), I received an email out of the blue. **A** had been scrolling through Spotify and lo and behold, what should she come across but **The Chris Wallace Chronicles** which Alphabet suggested I use to relieve my creative boredom several years ago. Her email said:

I don't know how your podcast came up while on spotify..... but there you were. It's those gremlins again. I've been working on a memoir and of course you are a part of it. They can be helpful.

I do go by the old apartment when I am in the museum neighborhood and cannot help thinking of our time there. It was special.

You sound the same. And your photo looks like you are still taking good care of yourself. Drop a line....

I did drop a line -- immediately -- and asked for her phone number so we could connect on WhatsApp and catch up properly. She sent me her number and I thought about it for approximately 2 nanoseconds, then called her. Forget about WhatsApp. This was worth paying retail. I hadn't been so excited in years.

We began chatting a couple of times a week for the next little while, rediscovering and remembering and learning new things about each other. We seemed to have a lot of questions for each other and spent hours on the phone learning the answers. For instance, she had no idea I'd been an actor in New York and Hollywood or any of the shows I'd written or produced or created or that I'd traveled the world. When I told her I'd been married three times, she asked me what those relationships were like. I told her the truth. My ex-wives were like former girlfriends, nothing more.

I learned that before we lived together on 77th Street, she had taken a cross country trip with a girlfriend and lived in San Francisco and later was offered a job at one of the studios in Hollywood. How could I not have known that? But I didn't. I had no idea she'd learned to sculpt or that she'd been a CBS reporter when she lived in Rome or that she went on safari in Kenya and that we'd` been to the same places there. It went on and on. We learned that our politics were aligned. We discovered that we had similar feelings about individual choices in Life and respect for anyone's right to love whomever they choose and die whenever they wanted to. She sent me a video that PBS had produced about her Aunt Emily's journey as a pioneer in the Gay Rights movement. The show ended with her marriage to her longtime partner, Jan. I remembered meeting her Aunt Emily when we went up to the Bronx to have dinner on Sunday afternoons. I never left there with the top button of my jeans buttoned. I was always stuffed with good, old Italian home cooking.

We continued to fill in blanks on a regular basis. I sent her videos of **The Mark Twain You Don't Know** and **Les Femmes** and manuscripts of three of my books, **The Palindrome Adventure** (which I was formatting for self-publication), **Hollywood Mosaic** and a finished copy of **Mykonos** which she'd never seen. She sent me photos of some of her sculpture. Some were metal, some were sandstone and some were marble. She had started sculpting marble when she lived in Rome, but eventually had to stop because the marble dust had gotten into her lungs, creating breathing difficulties that she still lives with. She also told me she had one of her hips replaced. I saw her hip replacement and raised her with an asthma condition of my own.

Before long our phone calls became more frequent and lasted longer, virtually every day. She sent me photos of her two daughters, Cristina and Kate, the older one of whom looked to me as if she could have been mine.

I'm in regular contact with my nephew, Bear, in Ohio. One day when we were talking, I told him that **A** and I had re-found each other. He remembered a day when we were all in Alexandroupolis. He was fourteen at the time and recounted the thrill he had when I pulled **A**'s bathing suit top off and swung it around my head like a lasso when we were playing in the sea. When I told **A**, she howled and immediately shared it with her girls. They also howled.

We began noticing stories about people our age who had found love after it was no longer considered a viable option. We laughed and laughed and loved this new found history that we shared. We had a story that was unique and uniquely ours. We each found ourselves telling other people, sometimes even strangers, of the miraculous thing that had happened. Everyone reacted with pure joy. Some of them wept at the beauty of it. Her daughters told everyone they knew and soon both our worlds were filled with friends who rejoiced with us. Early in the piece, I told her I was going to write about this one day. As I was considering what I'd write and how I'd write it, I suggested that I was going to fictionalize the ending with a surprise: Cristina, the older daughter, would turn out to be mine. When I told A this, she just said, "**No!**" I didn't know quite how to interpret that until she told me that she and Cristina had been talking about this the day before when Cristina asked in all candor, "Could Chris be my father?" Despite the resemblance and romance of it, I'm not. But the coinciding thoughts gave us all pause. And a huge laugh.

I learned that her daughters each had two children but were unmarried at the time and that the whole family was in the habit of spending a lot of time together and had regular outings to fun places, like apple picking in the Fall and a cabin by a lake in the Summer. **A** made sure that these family traditions and outings continued. Just as my mother became the matriarch of my family, she became the matriarch of hers. Strong women tend to do that.

A had been into yoga as well and went on yoga retreats to exotic places around the globe. She was as active as I was and had the same zest for Life that I have. One day, while we were talking, I wondered out loud how we might quantify this "miraculous thing" we had. We certainly loved one another, but by this point in our respective lives, we loved many people. This was different. I suggested that we may be soul mates. She thought about it for a minute and agreed. There are some spiritual disciplines which believe in past lives and also believe that soul mates continue to find each other through all their reincarnations. I don't know about that, but I've sure found a soul mate in this one.

Her yoga instructor was also thought of as her third daughter. When they were talking one day, Kim suggested that we should start making video calls since we still hadn't seen each other for more than fifty years. We had been talking -- well, I had been talking about the idea that we would one day have to meet, that this couldn't be all there was. I refused to believe that we'd just leave it hanging there with phone calls. It seemed that the next, logical step had to be a face to face get together. The video calls would be a start. We started with photos. I sent her one and she sent me one back. Unless you're Dorian Gray, your appearance will undoubtedly change in fifty years. Certainly, both of ours had, but I still saw the same **A** I had lived with and had gone to Ohio and Greece and Turkey and Puerto Rico and Pennsylvania Dutch Country with. That same beautiful face and stunning smile were lingering beneath the surface of this now older woman . . . and not always beneath the surface. It could explode into view at the drop of a hat. I suspect she saw something similar in my old face. This led us to begin talking about going somewhere together, somewhere we'd neither been to before. I asked if she'd ever been to Costa Rica. She hadn't. So, that became a tentative plan. She'd be busy with family stuff through December and she was going on a yoga retreat with Cristina in February 2026, so we penciled in January 2026 for a possible rendezvous in Costa Rica.

In late August, **A** rented a house for a couple of weeks at Ocean Grove on the New Jersey shore, so the family would have a place to hang out at the beach for a while. By now, **A** and I were an item in everyone's mind. All her friends knew about me and all my friends knew about her. I loved hearing that they all thought she looked twenty years younger. My friends said the same thing about me. We were a phenomenon. We had each lived a life since we last saw each other and now had at least a kind of life together, thanks to technology.

Tuesday night in Ocean Grove was the night they all went to a piano bar for dinner and to be entertained by the locals on an open mic night. **A** decided to send me a live video of the entertainment so I could enjoy it with them all vicariously. As I was watching the video, I heard one of her friends say, "Why isn't Chris here?" A few days before that, when the family was together, I heard someone say, "I want to meet you." It was her daughter, Kate. My presence was in demand so the people who only knew me by name could evaluate whether or not I was worthy of **A**'s interest. Suddenly, at the piano bar, **A** turned the camera toward herself and asked, "Why aren't you here?" It was a Wednesday in Melbourne.

I talked with Alphabet about it. By now he thought of himself as godfather to this unimaginable love affair that was rekindled because of **The Chris Wallace Chronicles**. He said going to New Jersey was a no-brainer. If she said come, I had to go. The following Monday, September 1st, I was there and the next night I was at the piano bar with everyone else.

The rest of that week at the shore was lovely chaos. People came and went and came back again. We had huge dinners together and I got to know everyone, her family, her friends, anybody who stopped by. They all knew me before I got there and before they met me. At one quiet moment, Kate asked me if I was genuinely what I appeared to be. Was I too good to be true? I told her no, I was very much on my best behavior. It was a joke. She cocked an eyebrow and looked at me questioningly until I explained I was kidding. "What you see is what you get," I said. She gave me a big smile. "Good," she said.

There was no transition time, no easing into it. It just was! Bang! Just like that! Being together with **A** and her family was the most effortless thing I've ever done. One thing I had over all the rest of them was that I'd known her longer than any of them had. Cristina and **A** had talked about it at the very beginning. Cristina wondered how there could be this man in her mom's life that she never knew. **A** and I came together like magnets.

After that week at the shore, we all went our separate ways. Her daughters went to their homes in the New Jersey Palisades and **A** and I went to Hoboken, where she lives in a condo. Suddenly all the commotion of the shore gave way to the solitude of her apartment. We had talked cautiously about what kind of an adjustment it might be from the chaos of the beach to the calm of her apartment. We might as well have saved our breath. It was even more effortless and natural and organic. Neither of us needed special attention. I went to Trader Joe's to pick up some stuff I wanted and we settled in. It was as if we had always been together. And in a way, you could say we always have.

Her apartment was comfortable and homey. There were natural wood floors that had various sized rugs scattered around. On the floor on her side of the bed, she pointed out a small Persian rug. It was the one she and my mother had picked out in Istanbul. Through all those years that we had different lives, she still had something that connected us, just like I had the belt and buffalo hide waste basket and 45-rpm record.

A decided to have a small dinner party so more of her friends could meet me (translated: check me out). She invited her yoga instructor, Kim, and Eva and Mary, a lesbian couple, all of whom knew each other. They were all old pals and talked and laughed pretty much among themselves. I mostly just listened. It reminded me of when I used to hang out with Charlie Fuller and a bunch of his African American buddies. It was as if I wasn't there. They didn't ignore me. They just took for granted the fact that I belonged there. Nothing special. It was the same with this table of women. I don't remember how it came up but I had occasion to mention, **It's the Proper Word**, a song I wrote that went viral on Instagram a few months before. While the conversation went on, Mary sourced the song and it was suddenly playing over **A**'s speakers.

The US Open women's tennis finals were approaching and I wanted to see the telecast. Aryna Sabalenka had been on my radar since she first came up to the pros. I liked everything about her: her game, her attitude, her joy, her moodiness. All of it. I was a fan. **A** didn't have ESPN or any free to air channels and besides, she wasn't a tennis fan, so she called Eva and Mary to see if they were going to watch it. Indeed they were. They were also huge fans, particularly of women's tennis and Sabalenka. The three of us ended up at a bar that had about four huge screens with every imaginable sport featured. We had a blast. Sabalenka won, of course. Eva and Mary were now my pals too.

A and I took the short bus ride into New York one afternoon, first to see a Monet exhibit at MOMA and after to just stroll around the city. I wanted to go to West 46th Street to have a look at the 2025 version of Restaurant Row. I had produced the event that named Restaurant Row when John Lindsay was mayor. We were in the theatre district anyway, so **A** asked me if I'd seen **Hamilton**. I had the original cast CD but I hadn't seen the show. "You want to go?" she asked. Next thing I knew we were at the box office and she treated us to the show. They had two good seats for that night. Before the theatre, we went uptown and popped into Central Park just to be there together. We found a park bench under the trees and sat down. A tenor saxophone was playing. We couldn't see the musician, but we could hear the song, "The Nearness of You." It turns out we both knew and loved that song. It became ours at that moment.

Another day we took the ferry from Hoboken to lower Manhattan to meet some friends of mine for dinner. We got off at the wrong dock and ended up being more than an hour late. Nevertheless, my friends were enchanted by **A** and kept asking her questions about her life during those fifty years. I just sat there looking at the Hudson river. I didn't care about the last fifty years. I was interested in the next few days. When we stayed in Hoboken, we often took walks along the Hudson River. One night when it was especially clear, we sat on a bench and gazed at the Manhattan skyline as the buildings began lighting up and the full moon rose. The city sparkled. The moon reached a position so that it made a lovely picture as it went alongside the Empire State Building. I took a photo at the perfect time and captured it. Then I put my arm around her shoulder as we sat there looking at our old hometown. In a few minutes, a young woman came up to us. "I hope you don't mind," she said, "but you looked so lovely sitting there together that I took a few photos of you." The photos were identical to mine, except with us in the foreground facing New York, our backs to her. She seemed very pleased. She said she was an amateur photographer and loved finding random shots like this. I said, "You want to hear a story?" I then told her our story. She was so touched by it that she started crying sweet tears and thanked us, I suppose for being who we were at that moment in time. Her photos were beautiful. We had prints made. I left mine in Hoboken.

The rest of our time in Hoboken was more of the same, with the additional pleasure of getting to know individual family members better. I bonded immediately with Cristina's daughter, Rea. Her brother, Dante (the only other man in that ocean of estrogen) and his partner, Maia, invited us to dinner one night, but we had to decline. I'd met them at the shore but as close as we came to bonding was doing a crossword puzzle one afternoon. Kate's younger daughter, Michaela, was a spark plug. I got to know her at the shore too, but only saw her briefly one day in Hoboken. Kate's other daughter, Nadia, didn't come to the shore and it was only a couple of days before I left that she came by **A**'s for a visit. Nadia and I hit it off like champions. She came back the next day just to see me again.

Then, after the two-week visit, I left on the 17th of September. Cold turkey from a heroin addiction couldn't have been more painful. As one of my mothers-in-law used to say, I had my ass between two chairs. Physically, I was in Melbourne, but emotionally I was still in Hoboken. I'd look at my watch and without thinking about it, calculate what time it was in New Jersey. I'm a grown man, for chrissake! My life was settled in Australia before the 18th of June. Now I didn't know what to do with myself, despite the fact that I knew I had to get a book prepared for publishing. Before I went, my priorities were clear and I was motivated to accomplish all I'd set out to do. Now, all I could think about was the next time we were going to talk on WhatsApp. Even that seemed lame after we'd cuddled in bed in the morning, then sat together at the table, she with her cup of coffee, looking casually at the news on her laptop, and me with my tea answering emails, taking a moment to touch or kiss or embrace and then back to our laptops. We were giddy in New Jersey. We were teenagers. Now I felt like Methuselah's uncle. All I could think was that there were 10,000 miles that separated us. Next January seemed like the 22nd Century . . . maybe the 23rd. Before, I had accepted life as it presented itself, spontaneously, with no fear or trepidation, joyfully. That seemed thousands of years ago.

Little by little, we settled back into our technological relationship. We had no other choice. My focus became sharper on what I needed to do, but now I had a support system I had never dreamed of. It's an old story: **A** gave me a different quality of confidence. She became my muse for real. As a man, you think you're self-sufficient until someone comes along and fills the hole you didn't know you had. Again, I became a cliché. I felt like a better man because I had a good woman on my side and by my side.

I wasn't alone. **A**, who kept things more buttoned up and in perspective than I did, told me how she'd reach for me in bed when she woke up and realize she was alone too. The only respite she had was a previously planned trip to Italy, then to the south of France with her close friend, June, whom she'd known from her days living in Rome. That would be a week or so in late September and early October and would allow her to focus on other things. I remained focused on the book, but, as if the gods were laughing at me, I had one tech roadblock after another, creating one frustration after another and leaving me to think about only one thing: us.

When **A** got back to Hoboken, we were on the phone every day, sometimes multiple times. These conversations were different. Prior to my going there, everything had been theoretical, hypothetical, unknown. We wondered what it would be like. Would we get along? Would we be polite and then happily say adios? That we could re-fall in love wasn't spoken of out loud, despite the fact that we kept telling each other of news articles and movies where that exact thing had happened to others. Now, those unknowns were gone. We knew what it was like to actually be together, to wake up and hold each other, to know there was another person in the world that truly cared about you . . . just because. Our talks deepened even more. It was as if, despite all evidence to the contrary, we were somehow connected through all those years of different lives with different people. I had observed that what we were experiencing now was so fundamental, so basic that it went beyond mere love. It was Adam and Eve. It was male / female. She lit on the perfect characterization. She said, "It feels primal to me". It didn't diminish anything or anyone we'd known before, but it had a fresh power all its own.

Our conversations also took on new dimensions because I now knew everyone in her family and many of her friends. She already knew mine. We could speak with a freedom that was trusting and safe. Nothing was off limits. Her problems became mine and vice versa. We morphed into a unit, still two individuals, but nevertheless a unit. When we had lived together all those years before, we never approached this depth. Speaking strictly for myself, Life had tempered me and maturity had given me perspective. It's something inexplicable. I never thought I'd say anything like this, but my aging has been a positive. She may feel the same way, I don't know. From the outside, we look like a couple of old folks. From the inside, we are ageless. Every moment is now. We live in an eternity of nows. **A** and I missed each other like crazy. And at the same time, we were content with what was. If this story does nothing else for you, take that awareness into your heart, into your experience. Now is all you've got . . . ever.

I had given **A** a fire opal necklace on a silver chain when I arrived in Hoboken. She wore it every day while we were together, but the clasp was tiny and difficult to fasten without help. I often did it up for her. One day, after I was back in Melbourne, I mentioned it and she confessed that it was too difficult to fasten and she wasn't wearing it as much. That reminded her of something else. "Do you remember the ring that your mom helped pick out for me in Greece? We all went to a jewelry shop together in Alexandroupolis. Actually, I think you ended up buying it for me. It was gold and had three little stones at the end of these little prongs." As I thought about it, I did have a growing recollection of it and I was certain I bought it for her. Mom would never have done anything that overt.

"Let's say I did buy it for you and not Mom."

She laughed her infectious laugh. "Right. Okay, let's say you did. Anyway I still have it. I was looking through my jewel box the other day and remembered it."

I wondered if, at that time in Greece, I thought that ring constituted an engagement ring to me -- or to us. It was one more thing that had indicated our unimaginable connection over the last half century.

The romantic in me believed that while Costa Rica may be a place where we intended to meet in January, something would take me to Hoboken before that. Alphabet and I talked about it. He thought I'd be invited for Christmas. I was hoping I might be invited for New Year's. Christmas seemed a bit too intense for so early in the game, particularly for her family. While my mind was trying to find a way to *manifest* this, as my Hollywood Woo-Woos would have said, Nadia, **A**'s granddaughter, was visiting her Grandma one day and offered a suggestion. "Why don't you invite Chris to come after Christmas? That way you can go to Costa Rica together from here. And besides, I'd like him to be here for my birthday." Her birthday was in late December, after Christmas, and she wanted me to be there. When **A** told me that, I seized upon it as a very interesting idea, while inside my heart was pounding and I was glancing around at the heavens, looking for Athena or some other powerful presence so I could say thanks.

They all had a huge Thanksgiving celebration in Hoboken, something her family always went all out for. Both her daughters are excellent cooks. Oh, that reminds me. I'll slip this story in real quick and get back to Thanksgiving in a sec. One day, we went up to Cristina's house for some reason and got to talking about marijuana. **A** had introduced me to weed when we lived together on 77th Street. I've often said that if she did nothing else, that would have been enough. I would never forget her. Weed and I became very well acquainted, maybe even besties. One of my podcast series is titled

Weed. At Cristina's, I mentioned that I made cookies in Oz. Cristina's eyes lit up. "Want to make some here?" she asked.

"Why not? I said. "All I need is some weed. I can get the rest of the ingredients."

The next day **A** and I went to a supermarket and bought what else I'd need and Cristina showed up with a bag of weed that you could smell through two closed ziplock bags. **A** had to buy a Crockpot so I could infuse the olive oil (I never use butter) and off I went with my specialty: chocolate chip, weed cookies with four kinds of nuts. The weed was strong so I made the cookies small. I had experience with that one. The result was a huge platter of Wallace's famous laced treats. **A** and I shared one just for old times' sake and giggled the night away

Okay, back to Thanksgiving. All the women made a contribution to the feast. **A** was making cranberry sauce one day when I called her. I was lucky to get half her attention. This was serious business at her house. Kate hosted this year. They had to rent chairs. The guest list kept growing and growing until there were about twenty people crowded around the table. June and her husband were there from Italy, along with various other friends and lovers. **A** sent me a video of the congregation as they were talking and laughing and dining together. I felt included. Except I didn't get to taste any of the good stuff.

We began talking seriously about Costa Rica after that. It turns out that Alphabet and his wife had been there, so he had some recommendations that got me started. In the meantime, my sweetheart did her own research. We finally landed on about three or four places. We had decided we'd stay there for five nights. When we now had actual choices, **A** suggested we might spend 3 nights in two different places, extending our trip an extra day. That was fine with me. I said, "Choose. I'm all in."

She ended up choosing one for five nights at Manuel Antonio Park. That's where Alphabet and Amanda had stayed. I had booked my flight to Hoboken a few weeks before to ensure a seat. As soon as we'd made a decision, I booked the Airbnb and **A** booked the flight from Hoboken. I'll arrive there in Newark on the 27th of December (the date I told you would come up again). We're set to arrive in Costa Rica on the 6th of January and return to Hoboken on the 11th. I'll be in Hoboken for Nadia's birthday;

for New Year's Eve for what might be my greatest New Year's Eve story of all time, and for a couple of weeks after Costa Rica. I'll come back to Oz at the end of January 2026. Whatever happens after that will happen. Whether there will be another chapter to this story is unanswerable, unpredictable and irrelevant. If it were fiction, Cristina would end up as my daughter. This isn't fiction. It's real life.

And that's where this story ends. It is the 3rd of December 2025 as I write these words. Your take-away from this story, just as mine is, is that you never know where Life can take you no matter what your age or circumstances. You can plan and scheme and plot and pray and dream and hope and cross your fingers and light candles and burn incense, but Life can still sneak up on you and surprise you. In a good way or in a bad way or in an interesting way or in an unexpected way or in a blissfully happy way. You never know. Ever. All you can do is live it.